TWICE BLESSED

TWICE BLESSED

*A Journey
of Hope
Through 9/11*

SHELLY GENOVESE CALHOUN

credo
house publishers

Published in the United States by Credo House Publishers,
a division of Credo Communications LLC, Grand Rapids, Michigan
credohousepublishers.com

ISBN: 978-1-62586-150-4

Cover and interior design by Frank Gutbrod
Editing by Elizabeth Banks

Printed in the United States of America

First Edition

To my Lord and Savior Jesus Christ

*Thank you for calling me into a deeper relationship
with You, growing me and not leaving me the same—
illuminating the steps of my broken path
and fulfilling the plans You had for my future.*

May this book be to Your glory!

To Jacqueline and Cash

*My precious gifts from God. I wrote this book
so that you would know how mighty the power of God
is to do more than we could hope for or
even imagine! Let this book be your reminder
of God's faithfulness—your stone of remembrance.*

CHAPTER 1

Train up a child in the way he should go:
and when he is old, he will not depart from it.

PROVERBS 22:6 KJV

This is not the story I would necessarily have written for my life; it's the story *God* wrote for my life. I could have spent a lifetime feeling sorry for myself when it didn't turn out the way I'd hoped, dreamed, and planned. Or, I could depend on an all-knowing God, whose ways are higher and better than anything I could've ever imagined for my life. God had a purpose for my broken path. This is my story.

I was raised in Garland, Texas, a middle-class suburb about thirty miles from Dallas. I had two loving parents and a younger brother named Price, who we all called Bubba. We were an extremely close-knit family, and I was a family girl through and through. Not a day went by that I didn't feel loved by others in my life. Our parents praised us often, were affectionate, and told us each day how much we were loved. My mom would put sweet little notes of affirmation in our school lunch boxes, and leave little gifts on our beds on a regular basis, just to remind us of her love. But most importantly, our parents spent precious time with us. This gave me a strong sense of security.

I grew up in an all-American neighborhood where everyone knew each other, and our neighbors were like extended family. I wouldn't say I was a tomboy, but I definitely wasn't afraid of hanging out with neighborhood boys or getting a little dirty. In the summertime, we would start the day off riding bikes, playing in a water hose, waiting for the ice cream man, and looking for neighborhood garage sales. Lemonade stands were a must on those hot summer days in Texas. My friends and I would bounce from house to house, and time seemed to move slower than it does today.

Our house had a screen door that was always open, and everyone was welcome there. My mom would make warm brownies and sweet tea if she wanted to lure us home. It always worked. She was a great homemaker, and I can remember coming in from playing after the sun went down to find good ol' home cooking: chicken-fried steak, mashed potatoes, and cabbage were always among my favorites, and it wouldn't be a Southern dinner without my mom's extra-sweet sweet tea, made with four heaping cups of sugar.

After dinner, we were quickly back outside to play hide-and-seek or flashlight tag or to catch fireflies.

It was an unbelievably simple time in life, and I wouldn't change a thing. We didn't have all the extracurricular activities kids have now; all it took to make us happy was the comfort of our family and friends.

Even as a child growing up, I was somewhat of a homebody. I loved being with my family. Home was where my family was, and I didn't want to be too far away. My mom was a stay-at-home mother and always made it look easy. She was the PTA president at my elementary school, cooked every meal in our home, and always kept the house pristine and organized. Her life was full, but she was always ready to make each day fun for us.

My dad owned an air conditioning company and traveled quite a bit. Since he wasn't always around, he wasn't a strong disciplinarian. He never raised his voice, he would give the shirt off his back to a perfect stranger, and he was the most optimistic person I've ever known. His fun, childlike demeanor made him a perfect fit for my mom, who was strong, compassionate, sweet as honey, generous, a great listener, and a bit feisty. She was magnetic, with a larger-than-life personality, and people always seemed to be drawn to her.

My mom—Debra Lea Dolan Pointer—grew up in a small town in Texas where she was the third of four children. She experienced a devastating event in her childhood when her older sister Diana, who she looked up to and adored, died of a high fever after open heart surgery. Sweet Diana was only seven years old. This tragic event caused intense heartbreak for my mother's entire family. Soon after this devastating loss, my mom's parents divorced. My grandmother spent many years searching for happiness, trying to fill the huge void in her heart, and working long hours day and night trying to support her family. She often had to leave the children to fend for themselves. Looking for love in all the wrong places, my grandmother eventually married several times. This was not an ideal situation for anyone, especially my mother.

My mom knew she wanted her life to turn out differently. As a young girl, she vowed to herself that she would never be divorced. She dreamed of finding true love that would last forever.

My mom had set her eyes on the prize at the young age of twelve, when she saw my dad for the first time at a local carnival. Mom's best friend, Kathy, was with her at the time, and my mom told Kathy that she was going to marry that boy. He was three years older, and his name was Ronnie Joe.

It turned out that Ronnie Joe was thinking about cute little Debbie as well.

Only four years later, Ronald Joe Pointer and Debra Lea Dolan were married. My mom was only sixteen and my dad nineteen. On the way to the church, my dad had a flat tire and started to have cold feet, but after fixing the flat and then driving around the church several times, he married my mom on August 9, 1969.

My mother had found the true love she'd always dreamed about. And just three years later, they started their own family—I was born on September 16, 1972. But having married so young, Mom found that life with Dad wasn't always the fairy tale she'd dreamed about. They faced some tough times. But they both had the same strong values about family, and no matter how difficult it may have been, they endured and always made it work.

Having her first child made my mom realize her purpose in life. Her most cherished job in life was being a mother. When I was a young baby, she would dote on me, dress me up, and take me out all over town to show me off. She was one proud mama. She had pictures made of me at Sears on a weekly basis, and they lined the walls of my childhood home.

When I was born, I had a head full of dark brown hair, and one of my eyes was swollen shut. I had to have a small surgery to open my tear duct. Even though I easily could have won an ugly baby contest, my mother insisted I was the most beautiful baby she'd ever seen. My dad would always strongly disagree, saying I looked like I'd been beat up in a boxing match. This, of course, would make Mom furious. This proves love is blind!

In the South, every mother thinks her children should be on a magazine cover, and my mother was no different. When I was just a toddler, she entered me in the Little Miss Duchess Dallas Pageant. This was our first experience with pageants. Lots of beautiful little girls were made up to look like mini adults—lots of makeup, hairspray, and frilly dresses. It was similar to what you'd expect to see on *Toddlers and Tiaras* on TV. The experience made my mother realize that maybe pageants were not a good fit for us.

When I was in kindergarten, my baby brother was born, Price Allen Pointer. There was no denying that Bubba was a beautiful baby. I loved having him to play with. I would dress him up in my doll clothes and stroll him around our neighborhood, pretending he was my child, but he didn't cooperate with this for long.

As Price grew up, everyone noticed that he was quick-witted and liked to make people laugh. Being raised in a neighborhood with a lot of older boys, he was taught things by them that he shouldn't have known. Don't get me wrong; he taught them some things as well. When he was only three years old, he would entertain us all by standing on the fireplace hearth telling jokes. Most of the jokes were a little inappropriate, especially at his age.

When I had friends over to spend the night, Bubba would run through the house naked—anything for a good laugh. He was adorable, but a mess, always getting in trouble for something.

Weekends were the best at our house. Almost every Friday night, going back as far I could remember, Fridays were what we called our Scooby-Doo Night. My brother and I camped out in our living room with my dad, and on Saturday morning we woke up early to watch cartoons together. These were precious times.

I was growing up, becoming very tall as well as lanky, and I had quite the imagination. I would look at myself in the bathroom mirror for hours, pretending I was doing a modeling shoot. When I was eight years old, I told my mother I wanted to be a model when I grew up. She encouraged me in this, telling me I could do anything I wanted to do.

That same year I signed with a local modeling agency in Dallas, the Townsend Agency. After I'd done some print work and had gone on a few commercial auditions, my mother and I concluded that being a model wasn't all fun and games. There was a lot of work involved.

It seemed that the talent I'd seen in the mirror needed some work. I started attending a commercial acting class at KD Studio in Dallas. After finishing the class, Mom and I decided we weren't quite ready to give so much of our time and energy to the world of modeling and acting. I think it made my mom realize that I would be a child for only a short time, and she didn't want me to feel like I'd been deprived of anything in my childhood. (And I didn't!)

My mom always made everything fun, making every day seem like a big party. Actually, she was the life of the party, and my friends always wanted to hang out at our house. She would stay up late at night hanging out with us and talking with us, and always taking us anywhere we wanted to go at any hour of the night. We made grocery store runs in the middle of the night just for ice cream or to rent a movie. I think she enjoyed my childhood as much as I did, since she was married so young and had to grow up fast.

She also was a great party planner. The parties were always over-the-top and entertaining. My friends and I can still remember them like they were yesterday. For one of my birthday parties, she hired several people from the community to judge a Dolly Parton look-alike contest. The party was complete with trophies, ribbons, big blonde wigs, and stuffed bras.

My childhood was incredible. But the most defining moment in my life would come when I was nine years old. An older woman, whose name was Melba, came to clean our house once a week. I looked forward to Melba coming each week because she was kind, sweet, and always joyful. She walked around the house singing and humming, and her joy was contagious.

Melba was a Christian. I followed her around our house as she cleaned, and she talked to me about Jesus. She told me how much He loved me. Of course, I'd heard this from songs like "Jesus Loves Me," but we weren't regularly attending church at this time in my life, so I was very curious about Jesus. God used Melba to show me how to ask Jesus into my life as my Lord and Savior.

Melba asked me one day if I'd ever asked Jesus into my heart. I hadn't, but I knew I wanted to, because I wanted to have what Melba had. She told me I needed to go somewhere to be alone with God, so I could talk to Him in private. I went to my parents' room and crawled inside their built-in dirty clothes hamper. I'd found a new secret hiding place. (It would soon become my special place to go and be with God.) That day, I crawled inside the dark hamper and simply talked to God. I still remember saying, "I want You to live inside my heart forever. I believe Jesus loves me and He died on the cross for me." Even though I was only nine years old, my life would forever be changed by a simple prayer and a sincere heart.

While I was growing up, my family usually attended church only on special occasions. We'd never really made it a priority to be there on Sunday mornings. It would be years before we started attending church on regular basis. So even though I'd accepted Christ as my Savior, I wasn't really growing in my relationship with Him, nor did I know much about the Bible.

That all changed a couple of years later when I was in seventh grade. One of my mom's closest friends, Melanie Ekblad, attended Midway Road Baptist Church. My mom adored Melanie and her sweet family, so when Melanie invited us to Friend Day at her church, Mom quickly accepted. Friend Day came, and we immediately fell in love with the church, the people, and everything about it. We felt at home. Instantly we were part of a new family. Our lives and relationship with Christ were about to change, all because we were invited to Friend Day.

Now we were at church every time the door was open—Sunday morning, Sunday nights, Wednesdays, and every potluck dinner in between. My mom's life was changing too, and she rededicated her life to the Lord when we first joined the church.

I immediately became involved in the church's small youth group. Our youth group was quite the motley crew. On Sunday mornings, there were usually about ten of us at the most. No one seemed to care if we were big or small, cool or dorky. Our youth group leader was young and fun, and he always made the Bible come alive to me.

I was growing quickly in my spiritual walk with Christ. The more time I spent in God's Word, the more I understood about Him, realizing what He had done for me on the cross and how much He loved me. Knowing this always made me desire to please God and want to obey His commands. I knew I could do things either the world's way or God's way. I constantly chose to do things God's way.

I looked forward to Sundays and to Wednesday night, but the highlight of my year was always church camp. I loved being surrounded by other teenagers who loved the Lord, praising Him together and feeling so close to Him. It was a mountaintop high, and I wanted it to last forever. I always came home from camp on fire for Christ and wanting to tell the world about Him. And I did! I was always very vocal about being a Christian and loving the Lord. I'm so thankful for those summers that always refueled my fire and reminded me to be a light for Christ in a dark world.

Having such a close relationship with a living God made my convictions of right and wrong much stronger than most teenagers. My brother, Price, didn't have the same feelings about church or church camp as I did. My mother had to drag him to church each Sunday, as he kicked, screamed, and cursed, hoping it would embarrass her enough in front of the congregation that she would leave him at home the following Sunday. But she always put her pride aside. She didn't care how bad he acted or how embarrassing he was; she just wanted him in church and hearing God's Word. I guess he eventually gave in, because my mother was strong and she was going to win the battle. I, on the other hand, was the rule follower, and I also knew that my mother wasn't going to let me get away with anything. She was the boss, and everyone knew it.

On the outside, to others, I'm sure it looked as though everything in life came easy to the Pointer family, but our family definitely wasn't perfect. We'd fallen on some hard times financially. With my dad being in the construction business, we often lived paycheck to paycheck. We had lots of peaks and lots of valleys.

By now my mother was strong in her relationship with Christ. She taught us to depend on God for all things, and that money did not bring happiness. When the money was good, that was great, but when my dad's paychecks weren't coming in, there were struggles. Lots of them.

My mother always wanted to make sure my brother and I weren't affected by the volatile times in my dad's business. She continued making sure we were always dressed to the nines, even if it meant her selling or pawning off her jewelry to get me a new dress for a school dance or any other special occasions. When my dad would get paid, we would return to the pawn shop and pray that her valuables were still there.

When my parents didn't have money in their checking account to pay our bills, my mom and I would go from grocery store to grocery store cashing personal checks, until we had enough money to pay for things we needed. Back then, the stores did not have the ability to know if there were funds in the account. My mom knew it would take three business days for the checks to clear the bank, and she hoped my dad's paychecks would come in on time. Sometimes the checks cleared the bank and sometimes they bounced.

My mom would do whatever it took to make sure her family was taken care of. When the large paychecks would come in, money would go fast, because we were always trying to play catch-up. My mom and dad were both extremely generous to everyone and would give our last dollar to anyone who needed it. And my mother always wanted my brother and I to have the best of everything, no matter if we had the money for it or not. We continued to live above our means. Month to month, the crazy cycle would start all over again.

I can remember several nights when I was rolling pennies, and we took them in to pay the electric bill in the middle of the night, so the electricity wouldn't be shut off the next morning. This was never a sad thing for my family; it had just become our way of living, and I didn't know the difference. We never longed for more, but we were trying to maintain what we had. Time and time again, I watched my mother give to the church even when we could barely pay our mortgage. But more importantly, I watched God provide for us again and again. We knew we had each other, and most of all, we knew that God was always going to supply all our needs.

One night when I was a teenager, I remember riding in the car with my family. We were all singing to the radio, laughing, and having a great time. The fabric lining in the roof of the car was stapled up to keep it from falling, we were probably driving on fumes, and we leaked oil at every stop. But I remember thinking, *How could anyone ever be as happy as we are?* My dad started to talk about some big job that was going to make us rich. I told them I didn't want to be rich, because I was afraid money would change us. I never wanted to change a thing. Rich or poor didn't matter as long as we were together. We were blessed.

I was sheltered, protected, and very naive. That might even be an understatement. I had a lot of friends in high school, but I didn't go to a lot of parties. Well, basically, I wasn't invited to parties. I don't think it was because I wasn't liked, but because everyone knew I was a "good girl." I never crossed the line on anything. Even when I got my car at sixteen. My mom would tell me not to go anywhere outside the Garland city limits, and I would literally make a U-turn at the city limit sign, every time I drove that far.

I had a close group of friends who were like-minded, who I'd known since childhood, and I also had my mother who was my very best friend. I didn't date a lot. I had the same boyfriend all throughout high school, a sweet Christian boy who respected me, my beliefs, and values.

I'm thankful that I became a Christian and had a strong relationship with Christ at an early age. It probably saved me on occasions from being tempted with teenage drinking and making other terrible personal choices that could have altered the path God had for my life.

I was a cheerleader my freshman and sophomore years in high school. At the end of my sophomore year, I tried out for varsity cheerleader, but I didn't make the varsity squad. I was devastated. I thought my world had come crashing down and my life was over. My mother realized there was more to life than being a cheerleader, although her heart was broken for me. She wrote me the sweetest poem. That poem, written for me while I was in high school, would become something I returned to often in my darkest hours that would come later in my life:

Trials (by Debra Pointer)
A disappointment may be what you're feeling today.
But be strong and thankful; God knows the right way.
He will open a window when He closes a door.
He's waiting to give you all you need and more.
There are people waiting to see what you will do.
Remember to tell them, "My Jesus will see me through."
Be strong in these trials and many more to come.
For your crowns are in heaven when all victories are won.

God had different plans for my life than being a cheerleader. That's when the door opened back up for me in the modeling industry.

I was in the Dallas Apparel Mart one day, when a striking young lady from a showroom approached me to ask if I was a model. She asked if I would be interested in modeling for her in her showroom. She was sweet, and I wasn't surprised to find out that she was a model herself. She told me I should call the local modeling agency in Dallas that she was represented by.

The next day I called them—the Stone Campbell Agency. I made an appointment to meet with the owner, Nancy Campbell.

Although I'd briefly modeled when I was child, my mom and I were still mostly clueless about the industry. As we walked into the Stone Campbell Agency, we noticed the walls were lined with head shots and magazine ads of beautiful models. Nancy was a doll, spunky and full of energy. She made my mother and I feel comfortable right away as we got to know one another in her office. Somehow Nancy saw through my big eighties hair, blue eye shadow, and red polka-dot dress that I wore with white hose and red high heels (yikes)! She saw something in me that she liked. That day I signed with Nancy Campbell, and she promised my mother she would take good care of me. My modeling career had restarted.

I soon had regular clients requesting me whenever they had something to shoot. Since I was still in high school, I wasn't able to work as much as I would have liked, but I was still able to build some great local accounts including JCPenney and Dillard's. I worked for showrooms at the Dallas Apparel Mart and was asked to do a special showing for department stores and other large accounts.

This was also the start of a new era (which would keep me super busy): shooting photos for Internet use. I had no idea what I was shooting for, nor did I understand who would even be seeing the photos on the Internet. This was in the early nineties, and at this time few people fully understood what the Internet would become.

The work seemed far from glamorous, but I was making great money and gaining much-needed independence. I was also meeting great friends while modeling. Everyone seemed to be a little older and definitely more street-smart than I was. The other models would teach me the ropes as we spent hours in the dressing rooms together in between changes. For me, I loved this new world. Getting to go to different places and meeting new people was a freedom I'd never really experienced, and it was exciting.

Some jobs were glamorous, involving beautiful clothing, cool locations, and makeup artists and stylists who were making the models perfect for the camera. Other jobs weren't so glamorous—like the many times I had to change in the backseat of my car in the middle of August, usually into a wool sweater. (Can you say *hot*?) But I definitely wasn't going to complain. I loved my job, and I couldn't believe I got paid do it.

In Dallas, modeling in the nineties included a lot of stiff competition. There were beautiful girls at every go-see and audition. My agency would call me and say a client was looking for a girl with brown hair and brown eyes, who was at least five-feet-ten. I would think, *Wow, she just described me perfectly*. I'd walk into the audition waiting area, and there would be at least twenty-five other models there who could have been my twin. I was always humbled to model, and I felt blessed to be able to do it.

At this time, most of my work was in the Dallas area. This was before we had navigation systems in our cars, and no one owned a cell phone, so my mom regularly went with me to my jobs and auditions. (Who am I kidding—she was overprotective and was always with me!) She would sit in the car waiting for me for hours while I worked.

I was ready for high school to be over. So, when everyone else started thinking about college, I started thinking about all the opportunities and unbelievable places I could go if I was able to model full time. I was starting to realize that I could actually have a full-time career as a model.

In 1991, I graduated from high school and was asked to be in the Miss Dallas 1992 pageant. My mom and I had always enjoyed watching pageants on TV, but I'd never really put much thought into being in one myself, especially after our limited experience with pageants when I was a toddler. At first, I was reluctant to enter the Miss Dallas competition, but it sounded like it was going to be a big deal. I thought it might even give my modeling career an extra boost. It was being advertised all over Dallas, on all the popular radio stations and in the newspapers. The pageant was to be held at the Loews Anatole Hotel. Bob Eubanks, who'd hosted *The Newlywed Show*, was going to be the MC for the evening. The judges would include notable lawyers, surgeons, and several people from the fashion industry, plus my favorite radio personality from Dallas, Kidd Kraddick. I was intrigued with all the hype and decided to go for it.

I ended up having a blast that week, as I competed against fifty contestants for the title—and I was thrilled to be named Miss Dallas 1992. This opened many new doors for me in the modeling industry and allowed me to get more involved in the community. I was in parades and on the radio, and I loved visiting the children at Scottish Rite Hospital, where I even helped light their Christmas tree for the holiday season.

After months of public appearances as Miss Dallas, a problem arose. Although this was a high-profile pageant, we found out that it didn't feed into the Miss USA /Universe pageant system, and that the "Miss Dallas" title had already been assigned to someone else to compete in the 1992 Miss Texas USA pageant. So even though I'd won thousands of dollars in cash and prizes in a prestigious Dallas pageant, and had been making public appearances and signing autographs for months, I wouldn't be able to have the Miss Dallas title to compete in the Miss Texas pageant. If I wanted to compete in the Miss Texas pageant, I would have to be assigned a different title. I was "given" the name "Miss East Texas" to compete at the state level.

The whole situation was confusing, frustrating, a bit humiliating, and most of all humbling. All my friends and family had attended the pageant and had watched as I was crowned "Miss Dallas." Now, suddenly, I was going to be on TV representing East Texas. I'm sure I could have made a stink about it, but that wasn't how I was raised, and what would I have gained? After all, I knew that my worth didn't come from any earthly title; my true worth was in Christ.

The following August, I competed in the Miss Texas USA pageant in Corpus Christi. This time, I didn't come home with the crown. I was definitely not seasoned enough at eighteen to hold the prestigious title of Miss Texas USA. But I did have an unbelievable time competing, and I made lasting memories I'll never forget. I met women who were beautiful both inside and out. But once and for all, I decided pageants were not for me.

It seemed like God was starting to open and close many doors in my life. I was discovering more about Jesus every day and learning how to trust God in both the good times and the bad, abiding in Him and trusting His ways.

CHAPTER 2

For the wages of sin is death;
but the gift of God is eternal life
through Jesus Christ our Lord.

ROMANS 6:23 KJV

A pparently, God had closed the doors for me on pageants and college, but He was opening the door wider for my career as a model.

I threw myself completely into it. While modeling, I was gaining worldly experience and meeting so many interesting people in the fashion industry. My client list had expanded, and I was working several days week. I was flown out of the country several times a year, picked up in limos, and treated like a queen. I did tea room modeling at the Mansion on Turtle Creek in Dallas, which I loved because I was able to interact with people. I was appearing in magazines, newspapers, and catalogs. I was traveling all over the world, and I was loving my life, a life I had always dreamed about.

My relationship with my mother and with God kept me grounded. I was always reminded that true beauty came from within, and that external beauty was fleeting. I continued to be humbled to have such an amazing job with unbelievable benefits.

By now, I definitely knew my way around Dallas. So my mom didn't have to chauffeur me around, but we missed our times together. On the days I wasn't working, Mom and I would take advantage of my time off, and we would go to lunch at one of our favorite places around town, and of course, do some shopping at TJ Maxx or Marshalls. My mom was only twenty years older than me and looked very young for her age. Most people assumed we were just girlfriends when they saw us together. People said we looked like we could be sisters, which was surprising, since my mom was five-three—with short blonde hair and green eyes—and (as my dad would say) "fluffy." She had struggled with her weight for years, but with her larger-than-life personality, no one seemed to care that she was overweight. By contrast, I had long dark hair and brown eyes, I was five-ten, and I had to maintain a healthy weight if I wanted to keep my job.

One day when I wasn't working, my mom and I went for lunch at Houston's, one of our favorite lunch spots in Dallas. A really attractive guy was sitting in a booth across from us and immediately caught my eye. Since I was at lunch with my mother, I didn't think for a moment that this guy and I would ever meet. But later, our waiter came over to our table and told us that someone had offered to pay for our lunch. That was a little exciting; it felt like something right out of the movies. Of course, I was hoping it was the attractive guy who I'd noticed. I asked the waiter to discreetly point out the person who wanted to take care of our bill—and yes, it was him!

I was super excited. I told the waiter, however, that I must decline the offer, but I wanted to personally thank the gentleman for his generosity (I just wanted the chance to talk with him). The waiter played the middleman, going over to give him my message. My heart almost stopped as the man approached our table. He was the most gorgeous guy I'd ever seen—jet-black hair, dark eyes, and a beautiful muscular body.

That's when I met Heath Calhoun for the first time. He was at lunch with his good friend Vance Miller. (Heath later told me that before he approached our table, he told Vance, "You be my wingman, and take the chubby one"—not knowing, of course, that the "chubby" one was my mother.) We asked the two them to join us.

I could tell right away that Heath had a playful and fun personality, an added bonus to his good looks. We had instant chemistry. As we got to know each other, I found out that he was a personal trainer at North Bodies in Highland Park, Texas. I told him I was a model, and that I believed he could model too. He played along with it modestly, and acted as if he knew nothing about the modeling industry. Eventually I found out he'd moved to Dallas from Arkansas because he'd signed with a modeling agency called Elite Dallas. He'd recently switched over to my agency, which was now called simply the Campbell Agency. Surprisingly in our industry, we'd never crossed paths before.

Heath told me he would love to take me out, and asked for my number. He'd definitely won over my mom with his quick-witted personality, and she'd wondered at once if there might be a little more to this meeting than simply a good-looking guy wanting to pay for our lunch.

I was nineteen at the time, and Heath was twenty-three. I was instantly infatuated by him. Immediately after leaving the restaurant, I called Nancy Campbell to find out the scoop on

Heath Calhoun. Heath did the same thing to find out about me. Nancy was a Mama Bear to all her models, always protecting us in every way. She made sure Heath knew that I was extremely close to my family, especially my mother; she also told him that I was a good Christian girl. I'm sure Nancy thought that we might not be the perfect match; she knew how naive and innocent I was. She also knew Heath was a very normal twenty-three-year-old guy who'd just moved to the big city from a small town. He wasn't looking to settle down; he was looking to have some fun.

It didn't take long for him to call and ask me out. On our first date, he took me to a place in the Dallas area called Deep Elm. The evening was fun because Heath was so down-to-earth and so easy to talk to. When the food arrived, I asked him if he would mind if I prayed before we ate our meal. I don't think he was accustomed to this on dates, but he definitely didn't mind.

When he was a baby, Heath had been adopted into a strong Christian home. He'd been raised by two godly parents and was a Christian himself. So, saying the blessing over food wasn't foreign to him but had never happened on a first date before.

Our lives were similar in some ways, but very different in others. He'd grown up in a small town in Arkansas of around seven hundred people. His family lived across the street from their church and were there every time the doors were open. He was just a good old country boy who had moved to the "big city" of Dallas.

On our second a date, we went back to Houston's. After a wonderful meal, Heath decided to order dessert for us. He ordered strawberries with whipped cream. Being playful, he picked up a strawberry, dipped it in whipped cream, and tried to feed it to me. I think he was seeing how I would react. He definitely got a reaction, because I was petrified! It made me quickly realize that we weren't on the same page. I excused myself from the table to go to the ladies' room, with every intent to call my mother on the pay phone. Thank goodness for the trusty quarter she always made sure I had with me! I was so embarrassed. I wanted to get out of that restaurant as quickly as I could.

I was playing with fire, because I went out with him again. We hung out on a few more occasions as friends. We never even kissed, except for a small kiss on the cheek in a photo booth. I think Heath respected me for being a good girl. He knew I was the marrying type.

Although we had a lot in common as well as undeniable chemistry, we were going different directions in life. We remained friends, and I even hired him to be my personal trainer for a couple of months. Who could blame me? He had an unbelievable personality and was easy to look at. This certainly wouldn't be the last time I would see Heath Calhoun.

I spent the next couple of years concentrating on my career. I went on a couple of dates, but never anything serious.

In 1995, I was asked to do a job for a New York City trading firm called Cantor Fitzgerald. They were holding their national sales meeting in Texas at one of Dallas's premier hotels, the Crescent Court. Their employees from around the country would be attending. A girlfriend of mine, Antoinette, who I'd known through the modeling industry, had a close friend who worked for Cantor Fitzgerald in the Dallas office. Her name was Nancy Miller, and she played a big role in planning this event for the company.

Since their employees had such high-stress jobs, Cantor Fitzgerald always tried to make things fun and entertaining at their national sales meeting. They wanted this meeting to have a "big Texas flair." My girlfriend and I were hired to be part of the event's opening meeting. We were outfitted in stereotypical western outfits: black leather fringe skirt, leather halter tops, cowboy boots, and a cowboy hat with guns in our hip holster. This wasn't my typical modeling job, but I was going to have fun with it. We entered the dark and packed room while the song "Bad to the Bone" played. A spotlight followed us as we walked down the center aisle toward the front of the room. We used the aisle as our runway as we played along with the rowdy crowd. Our job was to act like we were the bodyguards to the main speaker, who was from the Boston office.

The crowd was playfully cheering us on as we were pretending to shoot our guns and blow away smoke from the muzzle. Crazy and a little cheesy, but everyone was laughing and cheering and having fun with it.

At the end of the long aisle, I took my place on the left side of the stage facing the audience. As I continued to play my role, the meeting started. I noticed a man who walked in late. Everyone in the room seemed to know him. There were only a couple seats left, so he ended up on the row right in front of me. I enjoyed watching the crowd interact with him. I could tell he was charismatic and liked by everyone. I loved the confidence he showed, and his smile was infectious.

My heart was puttering. There was something special about him. Throughout the hour-long meeting, our eyes would occasionally meet, but then we would quickly look away. I knew I had to get to know this man.

When the meeting was over, my girlfriend and I made our dramatic exit. I quickly started inquiring about this magnetic man. In the hallway, I asked my girlfriend if she knew who he was. I said to her, "I think I'm in love!" Nancy Miller immediately knew who I was talking about. She told me the mystery man's name was Steven Genovese, and that everyone called him Steve or Stevie G.

I was right; there was something special about him. As she told me about Steve, her face lit up as she exclaimed what a great guy he was. He was tall, dark, and handsome, and looked a lot like JFK Jr. In his posture and manner, he projected great confidence, as if he was someone important. I quickly learned he worked in the New York office and had been with the firm since he was eighteen. He'd worked his way up and was now a partner with Cantor.

My modeling job was over for the day, but we'd been invited to have dinner with the company. I was super excited, because this might give me a chance to meet this man who so fascinated me. I showed up that night with the nineties signature model look—all black, head to toe—and with every intention of bumping into this Steve.

Throughout the evening, other various Cantor Fitzgerald men approached me, attempted to gain my attention. I gracefully declined their invitations to sit with them at dinner or dance, because I was boldly waiting on Steve to approach me.

Finally, Steve walked by, and our eyes met. My heart was beating so fast, but he was calm and collected. When he spoke to me, I could tell he was knowledgeable but without a big ego. He was so handsome, yet he didn't know it. He was cultured and well-traveled, yet made me feel important. I loved the way he carried himself. He was so confident and comfortable in conversation, always making eye contact with anticipation of every word I said.

I'm sure that I seemed uncomfortable. He was so refined, while I was so young, lacking in worldly wisdom. I truly had never been around anyone like this before. I didn't even know what to say. So, I told him he looked like Jerry Seinfeld. It was the first thing that came out of my mouth. Maybe I thought he would think I was cool for watching *Seinfeld*, since the show was about New Yorkers. Who knows what I was thinking? I'm not sure if he thought it was a compliment. He was kind and chuckled and said he'd never gotten that before.

I was immediately so taken by Steve. He didn't seem to mind my awkward and nervous attempts at conversation. Although he had so much going for him, you could tell he wasn't a player, but a great man who made me feel like I was the only person in the room.

We talked and danced the night away. As the night went on, I started to lose my nervous edge and acted more like myself. He made me feel at ease and so comfortable in his presence. I found out that he'd spent his childhood in Bridgewater, New Jersey. He now lived in Basking Ridge, only miles away from where he'd grown up. He traveled into New York City every day for work.

I told him that I would be in New York City the following month to work a swimsuit market. His demeanor changed. He lit up with excitement, and he told me he would love to show me the city. At that moment, I could tell he was just as excited to get to know me as I was to get to know him.

I didn't want the night to end. Luckily for me, my girlfriend and I already had a room in the Crescent Court Hotel for the night. Everyone was headed to an after-party in the penthouse at the hotel, and we were invited. I hadn't been to many parties in my lifetime, but I wasn't going to miss this one—just to be able to spend any amount of time with this unbelievable man.

The penthouse was amazing, like nothing I'd ever seen. The room was packed with Cantor Fitzgerald employees, mostly men. I felt like I'd just walked into a high-end fraternity house. Lots of handsome, young, and very successful guys partying and having the time of their life. I'm sure I looked like a deer in the headlights. I'd just never been to a party like this before. Even with everything going on around us, it was as if time stood still as I was sitting on the couch talking with Steve. We ended the night with hopes of seeing each other the following month in New York City.

Steve Genovese had blown me away! I knew from the moment I saw him that I wanted to know him and be part of his world.

Waking up the next morning, I still had butterflies in my stomach just thinking about him. I couldn't believe I'd met this incredible man. I knew this feeling was different from anything I'd ever felt, and it was something special. There was such an amazing feeling of excitement about seeing where this was going to go.

When Steve returned to New Jersey, we began exchanging letters and phone calls. Day after day, with every phone call, we became closer. (This was long before Facetime, texting, and emails were used to communicate.) We would talk on the phone every night for hours, getting to know each other. We were looking forward to seeing one another again, and planning all the fun and exciting things we would be able to do in New York City together.

After weeks of anticipation, the unimaginable happened. My job in New York City was canceled. I wasn't sure when or if I would ever see Steve again. I was beyond disappointed.

When I told Steve, I knew that he was just as disappointed as I was, but he was determined to see me again. He wasted no time. He called my mom to ask her if she would check my schedule for the weekend. He wanted to fly to Dallas to surprise me. My mom agreed not to tell me about the big surprise. She made sure I didn't overbook myself so I'd have plenty of time to spend with Steve while he was in town.

Saturday morning came. I was pretty bummed. This was the weekend I was supposed to be seeing Steve in New York. I was still living at home with my parents. I thought it was a little odd that my mom got me out of bed bright and early that morning, insisting that I brush my teeth and wash my face. She said with a wink, "You never know when someone just might show up at your door." She wanted me to be surprised, but she also wanted me to be prepared. I'd always been so close to my mom, telling her everything, so she knew I really liked Steve.

Steve showed up at our door, handsome as ever, with a bouquet of beautiful roses. I was beyond excited to see him and I even acted surprised. He asked if he could spend the day with me and take me out to dinner. I said yes, of course. I was thrilled!

A couple of days earlier, I'd booked an informal shoot for a market showroom. I knew it wouldn't be a problem if Steve came along and watched. I worked for this client on a regular basis, and they'd been hearing about him for the past several weeks. They were more than excited to meet him. Steve went with me to the shoot that day, carried my bags in, and got to know everyone on the set. Of course, Steve was such a gentleman and so easy to talk to that everyone fell in love with him.

That evening, on our first official date, we went to a beautiful restaurant in Dallas called the Old Warsaw. When Steve showed up at my house to pick me up, he was so handsome. He looked like a million dollars in his Italian suit with his monogram French cuffs and cuff links. I was finding out that one of Steve's most wonderful qualities was his being a true gentleman in every way—chivalrous, caring, and treating women with respect. He made sure he opened the car door for me, pulled out my chair for me at dinner, and stood up as I went to the ladies' room.

There were many things on the menu that night that I had no idea what they were or how to pronounce. He explained everything to me as if he enjoyed teaching me. He was eight years older than me and definitely more sophisticated. Steve was so different from any man I'd ever known. After ordering a wonderful bottle of wine, we toasted to new adventures. This would be the beginning of many adventures and the start of a whirlwind romance.

I know that Steve's hard work and financial sense is how our story was able to come true. We were able to travel to see one another almost every weekend as we dated long distance. The first time Steve flew me to New York City for the weekend was both thrilling and romantic. I wanted to look perfect for him and actually wore hot rollers in my hair on the plane for over two hours. Right before we landed, I went to the restroom to take them out, and stepped off the plane to my future.

Every time Steve saw me, his smile filled the room. He would say, "Shelly René, you are a sight for sore eyes."

Steve showed me around New York City on that trip. We did all the touristy things—like riding the ferry to the Statue of Liberty and visiting the Empire State Building, Rockefeller Center, and Saint Patrick's Cathedral. Nothing was left off my list. I was thrilled to be with Steve, experiencing all these wonderful things with him. I'd been to New York before, but being with him made every moment magical. I was seeing the city in a whole new light. He knew I loved musical theater, so he took me to see all the Broadway plays we could cram into one weekend. He even set up a private tasting with the chef of the Park Avenue Café.

Steve had blown me away and exceeded my expectations of a fairy-tale romance. He enjoyed doing things for me and got pleasure from watching me do things for the first time. I was like a kid in a candy store—not expecting anything from him, because I wasn't used to such elaborate things, but it sure was fun to be treated like a queen!

On that trip, he also took me to the Twin Towers to show me where he worked. Steve joined thousands of employees and visitors each day who would rush into these two towers to work, shop, dine, or merely admire the grandeur of the place. I was truly impressed with these extraordinary buildings and what they represented. The amount of energy throughout the buildings was unbelievable to me.

Steve was incredibly proud of where he worked. I'd never been inside the towers, and I felt blessed to be inside them for the first time with him.

By the end of the weekend, we could barely pull ourselves away from one another. We'd been dating for only a short time, but after every moment we spent together, it seemed to get harder to say goodbye. We even had "our song" already that completely described our relationship: "I Could Fall in Love." And that was exactly what was happening.

Most weekends, Steve was flying to Dallas, racking up frequent flyer miles. He would hop on the first flight to Dallas on Friday after work and catch the last flight out on Sunday evening. He was even getting to know the flight attendants by name because he was flying so often.

When Steve was in Dallas, I showed him how I really lived and what made me happy. I took him to all my favorite places, including the State Fair of Texas, where I introduced him to Big Tex and of course, Fletcher's corny dogs. He loved every minute of it.

Every Sunday he was in town, we attended church together, always followed by a Texas-style lunch with large crowds of friends and family. For Steve, this meant experiencing church in an all-new way, since he'd been raised Catholic. He knew that my faith was the most important part of my life. My relationship with Christ made me who I was and the person he was falling in love with. He didn't care where we were as long as we were together. He enjoyed getting to know what made me tick. It was like we were from two different worlds, and we were having fun being able to enjoy them both.

I was learning so much more about this man. He had many close friends, new and old, some going back as far as his childhood, which said a lot about his character.

He loved riding motorcycles, and he owned several. He'd been riding motocross since he was young boy. He was a true thrill seeker in every aspect of his life. Steve was fearless, from motocross to zip-lining through New Zealand, jet skiing at the Jersey shore, scuba diving throughout the British West Indies, and skiing double black diamonds from Vermont to Colorado. His passion, love, and zeal for life also carried over to his job on the trading floor.

This was a man who could have a conversation with anyone. He enjoyed yearly trips to the Super Bowl with his buddies and could fit into any social setting. He could enjoy his favorite drink in the most prestigious restaurants and bars in New York City, as well as hang out in his garage or the local bar with his buddies. Steve was a true guy's guy, and yet such a gentleman. My family and friends noticed right away that he was an accomplished man who knew so much about the world, yet he was still humble and down to earth.

At this point in our relationship, nothing could keep us apart. Everyone could see we were mesmerized by one another. We'd quickly fallen in love. As always, I continued to pray for God's guidance in my life and my relationships. I wanted God to direct me in everything I did, and I wanted to always be in His will.

Steve had great respect for me, my morals, and my values. He always said that he'd never met anyone like me before. He never wanted to change who I was. Steve was always very understanding that I was keeping myself pure. He knew that it was my desire to remain a virgin until I was married, and he continued to respect that. We of course were no different from any other couple in love; we had desires and temptations. We just never allowed ourselves to be put in compromising situations that might have made us weak. This is why Steve spent more time in Dallas than I did in New Jersey; it meant less temptation. He *really* loved me!

Our relationship was moving quickly, and it was time for me to meet Steve's family. I headed to New Jersey to meet them. After Steve picked me up at the airport, he decided to stop by and show me where he lived. As we drove up to his house, I noticed haystacks, pumpkins, and mums in the front yard. Steve knew that fall was my favorite season, and for my warm welcome, he'd had these put out by a childhood friend who was also a landscaper. Once again, Steve had gone the extra mile.

His home was simple, very clean, and extremely organized. Steve made a great living and was a very smart businessman, yet he lived modestly. He was humble, not boastful or flashy at all about his earnings, nor pretentious.

That night we drove a couple townships over to Bridgewater, New Jersey, where Steve had grown up. Steve's parents were divorced, and his mother still lived in the house where she'd raised both Steve and his brother. As we were nearing his childhood home, Steve shared with me many childhood memories. It was a lovely neighborhood with homes that were colonial style in the beautiful Garden State.

I met his mother, Veronica—she went by Vera—as well as his brother John, who everyone called JJ. Vera had endured a harsh upbringing in Scotland. She was happy to have escaped that chapter of her life when she was barely old enough to come to America to live. She got a job on Wall Street as a typist, where she met Steve's father, John Gaetano Genovese, who was called Jack by everyone. Vera and Jack fell in love and were later married. After their children were born, Vera left her job on Wall Street to stay home and raise their boys.

She had a thick accent, a mix between Scottish and Jersey. She was a tiny woman, with blonde bobbed hair perfectly in place, and fingernails that were well manicured with red polish. I didn't let her twin sweater set fool me; I could tell right away she was one tough cookie.

She wasn't at all like the Southern mothers I was accustomed to. She drank her hot tea and smoked her cigarette, as she put ashes into a silver vintage ashtray. She spoke highly about her sons, and you could tell she was very protective of them. She'd been through a lot, and it seemed like there was nothing this little woman couldn't do.

Steve told me stories about how she would often shovel snow from the sidewalk, then come in and prepared an amazing Italian feast. She would always make extra; in case anyone stopped by, she would be ready to entertain.

That evening, Vera was a perfect hostess and made me feel comfortable in her home.

It was also fun that night getting to know Steve's brother, JJ, because I'd heard so much about him. I could tell both brothers loved their mother dearly and took care of her. The Genovese boys were extremely close, best of friends in every way. Although JJ was one year older than Steve, it appeared to be the other way around. JJ had an outgoing personality and was having a good time joking around with me about me being so much younger than Steve, or as he would say, "busting my chops." JJ also worked on Wall Street. It appeared to me as though this was a family business, and this was the weekend I was about to meet the man who started it all: Steve's dad.

It seemed like Steve's dad was a legend on Wall Street. Everyone knew Jack Genovese. The boys had big shoes to fill, following in their father's footsteps. Steve and JJ always seem to aspire to the same height as their father. Jack was a man who saw great importance in teaching his boys a strong work ethic from a very young age. As a young boy, Steve had a paper route and later worked at a gas station. He'd learned to save his money. To the boys, Jack was a tough disciplinarian, giving his sons rigid rules and chores in order to teach them responsibility. He wanted them to understand that you get what you work for in this world.

This didn't go unnoticed by Steve. When he was growing up, weekends with his hard-working father were priceless to him. When he was in elementary school, his dad bought him his first motocross bike. Steve started to participate in motocross competitions around the surrounding area. He seemed to have a knack for this sport early on and became successful at it. He and his father began to spend their weekends traveling to motocross competitions, where Steve earned trophy after trophy. He and his father spent endless hours on the practice track, racing throughout the years. He learned the thrill of taking risks, jumping dusty hills, and getting back in the race after falling. This passion for excitement would draw him into living life to its fullest.

This was the father-son bond that he would carry into adulthood. I must say that I was nervous yet excited to meet this Wall Street giant I'd heard so much about. I met him in New York at a local bar called Johnny's, where all the Wall Street guys would hang out after work. As we walked in, I knew who he was immediately. He stood about six feet five, weighing well over 280 pounds, and looked like he stepped right out of a Mafia movie. But this gentle giant made me feel comfortable right away. I could see why Steve and his father had such a close bond.

After meeting Steve's family, I knew our relationship was moving forward fast. I couldn't believe I was already so in love with this man. After returning to Dallas, God started tugging at my heart, and I did some soul searching.

I knew without a doubt that I loved Steve. I loved who he was as a person. After only a couple of months of dating, I couldn't imagine my world without him in it. But I knew we were worlds apart in our beliefs. Although Steve had been attending church with my family and me all those Sunday mornings, I knew that he didn't have a personal relationship with Jesus Christ. Don't get me wrong, I loved that he'd been going to church with me, but I knew that going to church on Sunday mornings wasn't going to save him. Steve was raised Catholic, but to him Christianity was only a ritual, not a personal relationship with God. To me, it was something very different—it was knowing and depending on the living God every day for everything. This had nothing to do with Steve's religion, but it had everything to do with Steve's heart.

No doubt Steve was one of the best people I'd ever met, but I knew that God's Word said that it wasn't about "being good" but about knowing Jesus as Lord and Savior. I knew that if we were to get married one day, we must share the same beliefs. During our whirlwind courtship and falling in love so quickly, I somehow almost overlooked the most important quality I knew I needed and wanted in a husband.

I was devastated to think that this was a deal breaker for me personally. I wondered why God would put this unbelievable man in my life if he wasn't the one. I didn't know what to do, so I went back to what I knew best: prayer!

I started searching for answers in God's Word. Tucked away in my Bible, I found a handwritten piece of paper:

Top 10 Things I Want in a Husband
1. Christian (saved)
2. A man who loves me
3. Physical attraction
4. A strong desire to be with him
5. A man who takes charge, make plans and follows through with them
6. A man who is responsible
7. Loves children
8. Is adventurous
9. A man who likes to go new places and try new things
10. A man who enjoys being with my family, and whose family I enjoy being with

I'd written this list as a teenager, but it was as if I was describing Steve. He met and far exceeded everything on my list, with one exception—the first and most important item there.

I prayed about this, and talked to my mom. I knew how important it was to be equally yoked if we were to get married. The Holy Spirit had convicted me. I knew that Steve and I had to be like-minded in our faith before we could take our relationship any further. My soul was pained at the thought of not being with Steve, but I knew that being married to a man who didn't truly know Jesus as his Savior would not be God's perfect will for my life.

I was in turmoil as I continued to pray for Steve and for our relationship. It was so heavy on my heart. I couldn't keep it to myself. I started to open up to him about my convictions. The more we talked about it, the more my heart broke for him, because I knew the only true way to heaven was through Jesus Christ, who said, "I am the way and the truth and the life. No one comes to the Father except through me" (John 14:6 NIV). I knew without a shadow of a doubt that no one is saved by being a good person or by going to church, or by being Baptist, Catholic, Methodist, Presbyterian, or any other religion. It's *only* through the blood of Jesus.

Steve knew how important this was to me and had been listening all those Sunday mornings in church. He knew this wasn't a decision to make just to please me or have a future with me. This decision had to be made by him and for him.

Praying that Steve would realize that no matter how good we may be, we're all sinners and we need a Savior. As I continued to date him, knowing our relationship might have to end, I prayed and I set a date in my mind for Steve to make a decision about his relationship with Christ. This time frame was only between

God and me. I was holding on to God's faithfulness, knowing it would be painful to end my relationship with Steve, yet knowing God would bless me for being obedient to His Word. I never told Steve about my inner turmoil; I just left it up to God. I knew Steve's eyes would be open to the truth; I just prayed it would be sooner rather than later.

Soon, Steve started asking more and more questions about the Bible and about God. He was starting to understand that God desired to have a relationship with him.

The next weekend when he was in Dallas, we took a long walk after church and ended up by a creek bed near my parents' home. Steve told me he'd been doing a lot of thinking. He said he did believe that Jesus was the Son of God and had died on the cross for his sins, and he wanted to have a relationship with Him. He wanted to pray to ask Jesus into his life. He said, "Shelly René, I want you to know that I'm not doing this for you. Although I would do anything for you, I'm doing this for me."

We prayed together a simple prayer, and Steven Genovese asked Jesus Christ to be his Lord and Savior.

I don't think I've ever held anyone tighter; my joy was overflowing. My prayers had been answered!

Steve was always a wonderful man, a great humanitarian; but now Steven Gregory Genovese was also a *forgiven* man. He would return to New Jersey as a *changed* man. Not perfect, but forgiven. Now he had the assurance that he would one day spend eternity in heaven. He was later baptized at Midway Road Baptist Church in Dallas.

CHAPTER 3

For this reason a man shall leave his father and mother
and shall be joined to his wife,
and the two shall become one flesh.

EPHESIANS 5:31 NASB

M y thoughts were never far from Steve. I knew without a doubt that this was the man I wanted to spend the rest of my life with. It was so obvious to both of us that days or weekends spent together were never enough. Many tears were shed as we said our goodbyes each Sunday.

For me, the months that followed were spent writing love letters, sending pictures, and enjoying countless hours on the phone, many nights falling to sleep to the sound of his voice. We quickly started talking about marriage, children, and growing old together.

I would drop subtle hints to him by cutting out bridal pictures in magazines and pasting pictures of our faces on them (okay, so maybe not subtle). I was always sending him little surprises in the mail, such as homemade word puzzles made out of newspapers that he would have to unscramble to find the hidden message. He delighted in my childlike ways and even played along with my silly games.

I was so swept away by my love for Steve that I never thought about the fact that if I were to marry him, it would take me away from the only home I'd ever known and the family I was so close to. Nothing seemed to matter to me as long as I could be with Steve. He and I talked about what our future would look like together, about seeing the world together, and of course about how many children we wanted. I was naive to believe that one day, when we had a family of our own, Steve would somehow be able to leave his Wall Street job and move to Texas.

I truly didn't understand his job on Wall Street as an over-the-counter trader. In order to maintain the lifestyle Steve was accustomed to, he would need to be in the heart of New York's financial district. As we talked about this, he allowed me to believe that one day we could eventually move back to Dallas and raise a family. He knew that I was Southern through and through, and sold out to Texas, as any true Texan should be, brainwashed as a child to believe Texas was the biggest and best and the only place on Planet Earth to live! Steve was just as sold out to New Jersey; he thought that once I experienced everything the Northeast had to offer, I too would embrace his lifestyle.

My mother adored Steve because she knew he loved me and was going to take care of me in the ways that she had always cared for me. She also knew, as she watched us fall in love, that this meant I might one day soon be leaving Dallas. This was very difficult for her to think about. She'd spent her whole life making sure my life was everything she wished hers had been. I'd always been my mom's purpose. Her life revolved around me. Although she sincerely wanted me to be happy, she also wanted her baby and best friend to be close to home. She knew that my moving across the country would be difficult for both of us.

One Sunday while Steve was in Dallas, we took our traditional afternoon walk after church through my neighborhood. Sunday afternoons were always so difficult, knowing we wouldn't be able to see each other for another week. As we walked, we talked about his flight home, laughing about how he wished he could just put me in his suitcase and take me home with him. When we reached the creek bed near my home, he stopped and shocked me by dropping down on one knee. With the sweetest, most loving tone in his voice, he expressed his forever love for me. He told me he didn't want to live without me another day, and he asked me to marry him. He put on my finger the most beautiful and unique diamond engagement ring I'd ever seen.

I immediately said yes. I was overjoyed! All my dreams were coming true. Steve had the means to fly me to Paris or anywhere in the world to ask me to marry him, but he knew that the creek bed by my parents' house had to be the place. It was so special to both of us. It was the exact spot where he'd prayed and asked Jesus into his heart.

I couldn't wait to tell my parents, my friends, and the world. The minute we walked through the doors of my parents' home, everyone could see the glow on our faces. I held out my hand and we all celebrated. The man who met every desire of my heart, as written in my Bible years before, had asked me to be his wife. I felt like the luckiest girl in the world!

I didn't let any time go by in getting ready to be Steve's wife; I was ready! As I continued to work, I spent the following months planning our wedding with my mother. She and I were enjoying spending so much time together planning the big day.

Every minute spent with her was so precious to me. I knew that in just a matter of months, I would be moving across the country and joining my new husband. My mom was not only full of godly wisdom, but also so much fun to hang out with—a true best friend in every way. The quality time we were always able to enjoy was going to be missed.

I'd always pictured a winter wonderland wedding close to Christmas, my favorite holiday. And I knew I wanted to get married in the Crescent Court Hotel where I first laid eyes on Steve. When we met with the hotel's wedding coordinator, I found out that November 30 was available, and the hotel would already be decorated for the Christmas season. It was perfect. Everything was working out wonderfully. I enjoyed working to create a beautiful Christmas wedding, Texas style, including large groups of friends and family from both sides.

I was counting down the days—literally. When we were a hundred days from the wedding, I numbered index cards from one hundred all the way down to the day when we would say "I do," each with a reminder of how excited I was to become his wife.

The day couldn't come soon enough for either of us. My excitement continued in choosing a wedding gown, asking my friends to be bridesmaids, selecting invitations, tasting cake samples, and choosing the perfect flowers to make our wedding day amazing. It wasn't going to be an easy job finding the perfect dress; I'd modeled wedding gowns for years and had appeared in several bridal magazines, and I didn't want a dress I'd seen or modeled before. My mother and I decided to fly to New York to try to find the perfect gown. My future mother-in-law, Vera, met us for an exciting day of bridal shopping. I found the ideal dress for a winter wonderland wedding with a touch of white marabou fur. Steve was also very busy working, making our honeymoon arrangements, as well as preparing his home for me to move in with him after the wedding.

Finally, the weekend came that I felt like I'd waited for my entire life. It was November 30, 1996. The church was beautifully decorated with evergreen Christmas trees with white twinkling lights. It was a candlelight service, where family and friends gathered to rejoice and witness the exchanging of our vows. The organist began to play "O Holy Night." Steve took his place in front of the church along with his best man—his brother, JJ—and our pastor, "Brother Glenn" Meredith. Our wedding party of fourteen began their way down the aisle. My bridesmaids wore emerald green floor-length dresses that were off the shoulder, and carried bouquets of red roses. Steve's groomsmen were his closest friends since childhood. They wore formal tuxedos with bow ties and had small red rose boutonnieres.

As I waited anxiously, with my arm wrapped in my dad's, he turned and gave me a high five—just as he had when we were standing on the football field my senior year of high school, just after I'd been announced as homecoming queen. This had always been his way of saying, "I'm proud of you," and it always seemed to lighten the mood.

It all seemed so surreal as I stood behind the back doors waiting for them to open. I could have sprinted down that aisle to get to Steve.

The doors slowly opened, and the organist played the wedding march as our guests stood. I saw Steve looking back at me. He had the biggest smile on his face as he watched me walk toward him. I felt like I was floating rather than walking. Even though Steve knew there was no turning back, he also knew I was going to be leaving my home and a little piece of my heart in Texas.

As my dad and I reached the front of the church, he placed my hand into Steve's. We walked up to join our pastor. After we exchanged our vows, making a covenant relationship before God, my heart leaped for joy as we were introduced as Mr. and Mrs. Steven Gregory Genovese.

Our wedding reception took place there in the Crescent Court Hotel, in the very room where our eyes had first met. The room was lavishly decorated with beautiful Christmas décor—white flocked trees and poinsettias.

Steve and I took a special moment by ourselves to walk into the courtyard to look back into our wedding reception. As we embraced, we couldn't believe we were married!

Once again, we danced the night away, just as we had the first night we met, but this time as husband and wife.

Finally, it was time to say goodbye. Steve picked me up and carried me through the tunnel of a cheering crowd. As they threw red rose petals, we left the reception. Of course, it was no secret that I was a virgin, so everyone was really playing this up, cheering as we left down the long hallway.

We spent our first night as husband and wife in a beautiful suite at the Crescent Court. That night, as a wedding gift, Steve surprised me with a beautiful strand of pearls, and I gave Steve a poem I'd written for him. It was framed with a wedding portrait of myself, a gift he would treasure the rest of his life:

Who Says Dreams Don't Come True?
From the moment we met, I always knew
the knight in shining armor in my dreams was you.

There you were, what I had been looking for,
tall, dark, handsome, and oh, so much more.
When I looked into your eyes, it took me to a place I've
    never known,
only wishing and praying one day you'd be my own.
I could never begin to tell you just how I felt day,
but the way I feel right now has blown that feeling away.
God has truly blessed me; He must have loved us so
because He gave us one another and a lifetime for our
    love to grow.
So as I become your wife today, I give myself to you.
Because you are my forever love,
you've made my dreams come true.

The next morning, we were off to spend two unbelievable weeks in the British West Indies. Our first week was at the Four Seasons on the island of Nevis. This was paradise. I'd never seen or even imagined something so beautiful. The week that followed, we were in Anguilla and stayed at Cap Juluca, the most beautiful place on earth. The crystal clear, aqua-blue water was unreal. Sand dollars bigger than our hands would wash up on the pristine white beaches. And someone with white gloves served Steve and I champagne on the beach and spritzed our faces with Evian water. This had to be a dream; it was unbelievable to me! I had no idea people actually lived like this. God had blessed me with something so perfect, so unimaginable to this small-town girl.

While we were on our honeymoon, everything I owned was being moved across the country to Basking Ridge, New Jersey. After our honeymoon was over, I remember being on the plane, staring out the window, and finally realizing I wasn't going home.

My emotions were flooded with excitement, yet a huge part of me was scared to death of change. Home, friends, job, church—everything I'd ever known was about to change. I looked at Steve, and it was as if he knew exactly what I was thinking. He realized I'd truly never been away from home nor experienced much change in my life. He grabbed my hand and held it tight as he told me everything was going to be okay. He said he would take care me and make sure that I was happy.

I know it's crazy, but I was only twenty-three, and my heart ached as I felt a little homesick. This was the longest time I'd ever spent away from my family, and I was missing them, especially my mother. Steve told me I could go to Dallas anytime I wanted, and he would fly my mom in to see me whenever she wanted to come. (I thought Steve might live to regret this statement later.)

I was flooded with emotion. It was as if I was coming off a roller coaster ride. I'd been on a high for so long planning the wedding, getting married, then the two-week honeymoon. But this type of high couldn't last forever.

We had a car service pick us up at the airport and headed to Basking Ridge. As we pulled up to his house, I saw a beautiful black BMW waiting for me in the driveway with a big red bow on it. Inside was a note that said, "Welcome home."

CHAPTER 4

A friend loves at all times,

and a brother is born for a time of adversity.

PROVERBS 17:17 NIV

The following Monday, Steve returned to work in the North Tower of the World Trade Center. For me, everything was so exciting and new as I began to unpack, settling into my new home. Steve was used to getting up early, grabbing the *Wall Street Journal*, and heading to the train station for his one hour morning commute to New York City. Cantor Fitzgerald was the only firm Steve had ever worked for in his career on Wall Street. I'd heard many stories about his job and about Wall Street in general, and knew more than I wanted to know about money, trading, and the behind-the-scenes lifestyles.

Steve told me one story I would never forget—about when he escaped the 1993 terrorist bombing of the World Trade Center's North Tower. Steve and his colleagues in his office on the 104th floor were thankfully unharmed by the truck bomb beneath their building, and they joined thousands who rushed down smoke-filled stairways to evacuate. He said it took him three hours to finally reach the ground floor. It was hard for me to believe it had taken so long, but with the stairways being so congested with people, it made everyone panic. Steve said he was covered in black soot, as if he'd been climbing inside a chimney.

After he finally made it home, he showered, packed his bag, and headed to Vermont to go snow skiing for a couple of days. Knowing Steve, he probably had this weekend getaway planned, and nothing was stopping him from living life to the fullest and enjoying time with his buddies. Steve was a survivor.

Steve often told me that he knew his building was a target for terrorism because of what the towers represented to the world: the height of economic power. Along with most of the people working in the World Trade Center, he'd heard of Al-Qaeda long before the rest of America had. Steve said he wasn't fazed by that potential threat; he had a job to do that he loved, and he never expected he would ever be in real danger.

From the heinous act of violence in that 1993 attack, six innocent people died and over a thousand were injured. Thankfully, the perpetrators of the attack were later convicted in New York City and imprisoned.

Along with Steve's zeal for life, one thing that set him apart was his ability to make lasting friendships. He always enjoyed meeting new people.

It seemed to me that everyone who worked on Wall Street knew each other. They were like a big family. Long before I came into Steve's life, he met Mary Kay, a woman who commuted with him daily into the city. Mary Kay also worked on Wall Street, but for Lehman Brothers. Through the many years of train rides, she and Steve became close friends.

Steve later became friends with Mary Kay's husband, Bob, because of their shared love for motorcycles, especially Harleys. Mary Kay and Bob were among the first friends of Steve that I'd met before moving to New Jersey.

Mary Kay was a tiny little thing who was able to hold her own with these tough Wall Street guys. She was bold and definitely said what was on her mind. This New York–style personality was something I was going to have to get used to. I was so passive, but everyone I'd met seemed to have more straightforward personalities.

But there was more to Mary Kay, I quickly realized she also had a more nurturing side to her. She was a smart, hardworking mother of two, loved to work out, and could cook like a culinary chef. She knew right away that I was very naive and had a lot to learn. She took me under her wing, and we quickly became friends.

After settling in, I began modeling in New York City. Most of my jobs at first were through my contact with JCPenney back in Dallas. They'd sent all my information to their New York contacts, and my new agent started booking me right away. This work was such a blessing for me because it was something familiar. JCPenney booked me weeks in advance. And it was great to have jobs on the books without having to go on a ton of go-see's in New York. I was thrilled to be working in New York City, a dream of mine since childhood.

I looked forward to the days when I worked in the city because Steve and I were able to commute together. I just followed Steve's lead because I had no idea what I was doing or where I was going. The train station was less than a mile away from our house, and we enjoyed the homemade muffins and coffee that were sold at the small train station. It was so interesting to watch the people getting on and off the train at each stop. They all looked like they'd been commuting their whole lives.

The New Jersey Transit dropped us off under the World Trade Center, then Steve would walk me through the large building and put me in a cab that would take me to midtown for my day's work. After a long day, I'd rush back downtown so Steve and I could catch the train back to New Jersey together. On days when I only worked only a couple of hours, or just had go-see's, I would spend the rest of the day exploring. Steve and I would often have dinner together in the city, and occasionally see a Broadway show or do anything else our hearts desired. I was getting used to this new and exciting way of living.

One afternoon, after working for JCPenney, I realized I didn't have a dime on me to catch a cab to meet Steve downtown. And the walk was over fifty blocks. In 1996, cabs didn't take credit cards, and unfortunately that's all I had with me that day. I was too embarrassed to call Steve; he'd reminded me so many times not to forget to carry cash. And he was so extra protective of me that I didn't want him to worry.

I decided to be a big girl and figure out how to get some cash. I walked into Starbucks, where I noticed about fifteen people in line. I stood in the center of the room and spoke out loud to the customers by introducing myself and explaining to them that I needed cash to get downtown to meet my husband. I asked if anyone would be willing to let me pay for their drink with my credit card and give me cash in return. Most of the people in the room never even looked up or made eye contact! Maybe they thought I was homeless or crazy, but three customers in line did let me pay for their drinks, and I had enough money to make it downtown. My inner Southern girl was coming out, and I was starting to realize I wasn't in Texas anymore.

I had a lot to learn. I'd been so sheltered by my parents, especially by my mother. Even though I'd worked since I was sixteen, I never learned how to pay bills or even balance a checkbook. My mother had tried to teach me, but she thought it would make my life easier if she just did those things for me. While I lived at home, she'd done everything for me. Now that I was married to Steve, he would take over, and I was extremely happy about that. I had no real desire to be independent. Honestly, I liked not having a care in the world and having someone take care of me. It made me feel loved and secure. It was definitely my love language. Steve and my mother were alike in many ways, and this was one of them.

Christmas was around the corner, and Steve got a big kick out of me sending all his Jewish friends Christmas cards. I had no idea this wasn't politically correct. Honestly, it was hard to believe that not everyone celebrated Christmas. Yes, I had lived in a bubble! To my defense, we were not taught about different cultures in school when I was growing up.

On our Christmas card that year was a picture of Steve and me that was taken on a snow skiing trip at Beaver Creek in Colorado, along with a two-page letter about our new life together. I sent it out to all our family and friends as well as to Steve's business associates.

Steve was speechless when he realized what I'd done. He was *not* happy. His friends definitely gave him a hard time. Steve was a bit more private and thought the letter sounded pretentious. I was just overly ecstatic about everything that had happened in my life, and I wanted to share it with the world, especially my Texas friends.

We headed to Dallas for our first Christmas together. I loved being home for the holidays. My family was over-the-top about Christmas and had many Christmas traditions which included going out to dinner on Christmas Eve, wearing matching Christmas pajamas, and making a birthday cake for Jesus. Steve thought we were big dorks, but went along with all our traditions. That Christmas day, my dad gave Steve his first pair of cowboy boots. Steve was quite the sight on Christmas morning with his Christmas PJs and new cowboy boots.

After the holiday season, my days spent in New Jersey when I wasn't working were long, as I waited each day for Steve to come home. I would drive around trying to get to know the area and finding new things to do, but there was literally nothing around us. The closest mall or Starbucks was about thirty minutes away. With no navigation of any sort, I often got lost while I was exploring. I once ended up in Pennsylvania. I called Steve crying while I was sitting on the side of the road, wondering how I'd gotten so lost that I ended up in another state. I got lost almost weekly during the first few months. Steve was always so patient with me, helping me find my way back home.

I was eagerly trying to please Steve, with no real experience of being a homemaker. I was beginning to learn how Steve liked things done and how meticulous he was about everything. Steve made sure his garage was perfectly organized with labels on everything. Every different kind of nail and screw had its own glass container clearly marked. He liked his laundry done a certain way, and never wanted his T-shirts folded with a center crease. I was just happy my mother had taught me not to wash white towels together with blacks.

Honestly, I was quite the joke, though I'd turned his bachelor pad into a home—which Steve was really happy about. It was always clean, and I attempted to have a beautiful meal on the table when he got home from work. Most nights I set the table with beautiful linens and fresh flowers, a wonderful presentation, but he was just being nice to eat half the things I set in front of him. What was I thinking, cooking for an Italian? I worked hard to learn how to be a better cook. Steve's mother also taught me how to make some of his favorite Italian meals, such as homemade meatballs and manicotti. A Southern recipe that would quickly become one of Steve's favorites was strawberry bread. This recipe had been passed down from the mother of one of my childhood friends and was a favorite of mine. With practice, my meals were soon edible, though I was never going to live up to being a Genovese.

Thursday nights were our sushi night, and I didn't have to cook. We would head to a hole-in-the-wall sushi bar that Steve had been going to for years, meeting some of Steve's closest childhood friends there weekly. This was something we both looked forward to—not having to eat my cooking and going out! I was having fun getting to know Steve's friends, and they were quickly becoming my friends.

Thank goodness for the weekends. It was always my favorite time because New York and New Jersey were Steve's playground. He always knew where we could go to have a good time and I couldn't wait to spend every minute with him. Steve loved to ride his Harley and I loved to ride with him. We spent many afternoons riding along the hillsides of New Jersey. Or heading to New Hope, Pennsylvania, to have lunch, and do a little antique shopping. I loved feeling the wind in my face and being on the back of his motorcycle. He always made me feel so safe and secure. We took weekend trips to all his favorite places—Long Beach Island on the Jersey shore, Vermont, the Hamptons, or anywhere else in the world Steve wanted to show me. We were having the time of our lives and were more in love with each other than ever.

The first New Jersey snowfall I experienced was stunning, just magical. I wanted to go play outside, make snow angels, and build a giant snowman. Steve would appease me while trying to explain to me that there was a certain kind of snow that was better for packing. Who knew? I'd grown up in Texas, so when it snowed, which was rarely, we would collect snow from the entire neighborhood to make a community snowman. Now that I was living up north, I had to learn how to drive in the snow, shovel snow, dress for snow, and to always keep an ice scraper handy.

At first the snow was fun and beautiful to look at, but after months of cold winter days, being stuck in the house while Steve was working, I was over the cold weather!

After a long winter, the seasons finally began to change. I couldn't have been happier to see the sun again. I adored my new life, but I often felt like I was a fish out of water. Even though I was living the fairy tale I'd always dreamed about, there was something missing. Life in New Jersey was much different from how I'd grown up in the South, and I longed for familiarity. I missed my Southern roots; I missed Texas, my family, my friends, and my church. It had been nearly seven months, and I felt like I'd been on an unbelievable vacation, but now I wanted to know when I was going to get to go home.

Steve continued to assure me that one day he would move me back to Texas. I'm sure he regretted telling me this, because every time I started to get homesick, I would have him reassure me that one day we would be raising a family in Texas.

He tried to keep me busy when I wasn't working to keep my mind occupied. He even hired a college literature teacher to come to the house, and we had what I would call a book club. For me it was more like a rent-a-friend. At least I had someone to talk to during the day, even if it was about *The Scarlet Letter* or *To Kill a Mockingbird*.

I tried to find hobbies. I'd never had a real hobby. My idea of a hobby was shopping. I did a lot of this, but it was no fun shopping alone, and it only temporarily filled my void. I started taking equestrian horseback riding lessons, I joined a gym, and Steve even made me watering schedules for the yard just to keep me busy.

Steve never doubted how much I loved him, but he knew I was struggling with being homesick. I know that part of it was that I'd never been away from home for longer than a couple of weeks. I'd never gone to college and never experienced being away from my family. I was pitiful.

I talked to my mom several times a day. I'm sure it broke her heart to hear that I was so homesick. It never helped that she always sounded like she was having the time of her life going to lunch with all our closest friends at all our favorite places in Dallas.

I knew I desperately needed to have a close friend nearby, someone to confide in besides my mother. I started praying daily that I wouldn't be so homesick. I prayed specifically to meet Christian friends. I had so many close girlfriends in Texas who

I'd known practically all my life. I'd met many new friends in the Northeast, but something was still missing.

Steve recognized the importance of close friends. He had many, and always went out of his way to make every opportunity for us to get together with them. As a couple, we had lots of couple friends, but almost all the women in those couples worked during the day. I needed someone to go out with, to go to lunch with, to pray with, and to study the Bible with. I desperately needed a close friend in my life who was like-minded. I'd met outstanding people, but few who truly shared my convictions and beliefs.

One day I was going into New York City for a JCPenney booking. As I was getting out of the cab, I saw one of the most beautiful women I'd ever seen. She was walking into the same building I was about to enter. I knew right away she was a model. Her skin was porcelain and flawless. She was tall, thin, and had beautiful long blonde hair.

Inside, we rode up on the same elevator together and realized we were heading to the same job. I'd been working for JCPenney for several months and had never seen her before. The clients usually hired the same models week after week, but she was new.

In the dressing room, we started talking. I could tell immediately that she was a Christian and loved the Lord. I was so excited to meet someone I had so much in common with. I was mesmerized by her poise and her knowledge. We went to lunch together that day and instantly became friends.

This was the first time I met Lizabeth Johnson. She was simply exquisite in so many ways. Everything about her, inside and out, was beautiful. She'd been with the top modeling agencies in New York and overseas for years. This day's JCPenney job paid very well, but it was beneath her usual pay scale. She later said she didn't know why she took this particular job, but we both could look back and see that it was God-ordained. Once again, God had answered my prayers.

We quickly became close friends and began to spend time together. Steve was thrilled that I'd met a friend to spend quality time with on a regular basis.

Steve soon met Lizabeth's husband, Richard, who also worked in the financial industry. They got along great and had a lot in common. We began to spend time with them as a couple.

During the week I would visit Lizabeth at her home in Connecticut, and we would spend the day together. Connecticut was two hours away but worth the drive, because I loved spending time with her. She was seasoned in her walk with Christ and had so much biblical knowledge. She seemed to have everything together. She prayed beautifully with power and had Scripture to back up everything that came out of her mouth.

Lizabeth became such a true friend, and helped ease my pain of being homesick. God had not only sent me a precious friend but a true mentor in Christ.

I began to realize that not only had I needed a close friend, but we needed to find a church home. For several months, we would visit nearby churches. It was a lot different from the South, where you could find a church on every corner. We weren't looking for any special denomination, but just a church where we could go and grow in our relationship with Christ.

While searching, we experienced many different kinds of church services and worship. We tried several different churches, but we were having a hard time finding a good fit.

One Sunday morning, I remember visiting a local nondenominational church. Everyone was super nice, and they were exceptionally welcoming. We took our seats, and as the worship service began, everyone reached under the chairs and pulled out tambourines. Steve looked at me, and I'm sure he was thinking, *Where have you brought me?* They were all just singing and shaking their tambourines. For Steve, this was definitely out of his comfort zone. I'd never experienced this type of worship, growing up Baptist, but I wasn't opposed to it. This was their way of praising the Lord, and that was good with me. But I also wanted Steve to be comfortable.

The next weekend we visited Millington Baptist Church. This was a great fit for both Steve and me. Now we had a church to call our own.

I would love to say that I jumped right in and got involved in the church, but our weekends always seemed so busy. I was at that age in life where everyone was getting married and starting their families. There was always some sort of bridal or baby shower going on back home, and I started traveling back to Dallas several times a month. This meant weekends away from Steve and not being in church together. Steve never seem to mind me going to Dallas as long as it made me happy. He'd been a bachelor for so many years that a couple of days away from me never seemed to bother him. While I was in Dallas he spent his weekends with his buddies, hanging out at the local bar watching sports, throwing darts, or riding motocross.

My homesickness had finally gone away, and I was happy and content with our busy lifestyle. I eventually just gave in to the fact that I might not be going back to Dallas to live anytime soon. I was okay with that, because by now I had many close girlfriends and a life of my own in New Jersey. I still missed Texas, but I had Steve and the best of both worlds—all the perks of living in the Northeast and I could hop on a flight to Dallas anytime I wished.

After three blissful years of marriage, Steve was ready to move from his starter home. We thought it would be a great idea to build a home together. He felt like this would really make New Jersey feel like home to me. I totally agreed, and I was so excited to start the process.

I'd been cutting pictures out of magazine for years for design ideas for our dream home. On weekends we would drive around looking at what was for sale or just to get ideas. We looked at several homes but nothing felt right.

We drove past a beautiful home that looked like a castle from the outside, and I fell in love with it. But this house wasn't on the market. For weeks afterward, during the day while Steve was at work, I would drive past the house trying to soak in every detail large and small. One day I finally got up enough courage to walk up to the front door. A lady answered the door, and I learned that she was the owner. I told her how much I adored her unique home, and I asked her if I could have a tour. Looking back, I can see that this was practically insane, but I was bound and determined to see the inside of this castle I'd fallen in love with. She wasn't even skeptical of this Texas girl with a thick accent; she was so kind, giving me a personal tour. She also gave me the names of the architects who designed the house.

I was so excited, I immediately called Steve. Soon we had house plans that we would tweak to fit our needs. All we needed now was a piece of land to build it on. We loved Basking Ridge, so we started looking there. We were looking for a large lot with space not only for our home, but also for outdoor entertaining.

It didn't take long for us to find the perfect location, only a few miles from where we'd been living. We found a builder, and we were excited that he and his wife were going to be our new next-door neighbors.

After closing on the lot, Steve and I both felt extremely blessed to have found such an unbelievable property. We went straight to our new piece of land and prayed, thanking God for the many blessings He'd given us.

And now it was time to start a family.

CHAPTER 5

*From his abundance we have all received
one gracious blessing after another.*

JOHN 1:16 NLT

When I found out that I was pregnant, I was overjoyed! I could barely keep the news to myself. I couldn't wait to tell Steve! I wanted it to be in person and in a very special way. I rushed to the store and found the cutest little book: *How to Pamper Your Pregnant Wife*. While he was at work, I videotaped myself holding up my pregnancy test, telling him we were going to have a baby.

The day seemed longer than normal, waiting for Steve to come home from work and trying not to blurt out the exciting news over the phone. I wrapped the book, placed the videotape beside it, and laid it on the kitchen counter for Steve to see when he walked through the door.

Steve loved surprises. As he walked into the kitchen and saw the gift lying on the counter, he already had a grin on his face. As he slowly unwrapped the book, I could tell what he was thinking. He read the title out loud, then said, "Shelly René, are we going to have a baby?" I smiled as we embraced and played the videotape. We laughed and rejoiced together in the special gift God was giving us both.

There were so many unbelievable things going on in our lives, but the most thrilling was expecting our first baby. We were overjoyed and couldn't wait to tell the world our news. We immediately called both our families and some of our closest friends.

Steve and I were especially eager to tell our special friends Lizabeth and Richard. We were scheduled to have dinner with them in New York City, where we would tell them our great news. That night we both had something to share. Lizabeth and I were both expecting babies! Both in May! I couldn't have been more thrilled to share such a special time in my life with one of my newest and closest friends.

I loved being pregnant. I honestly embraced the changing of my body. It felt like my life could not get any better.

We eagerly looked forward to finding out if we were going to have a girl or a boy. When it was time to find out the baby's sex, we asked the doctor to write it down on a piece of paper and to seal it in an envelope, for us to open later. We were going to open it on Christmas morning with my family in Dallas. We did just that. On Christmas morning, we ripped open the envelope that we'd been holding onto for weeks. We found out we could start painting our nursery pink. We were going to have a baby girl!—a dream come true.

I continued to model in New York City, trying to keep my pregnancy a secret until I was five months pregnant. I stayed busy picking out items for our new home, including crown molding, appliances, chandeliers, and paint colors. But the most exciting job was decorating the sweetest baby room ever.

Steve was doing a great job of pampering me. We enjoyed taking Polaroid pictures of my expanding belly and comparing them to the month before. This baby was already so loved before she even took her first breath. We would read to her and sing to her, and most importantly, pray for her daily.

Before we knew it, the time had come for our sweet angel to be born. On May 10, 2000, she arrived: Jacqueline Lea Genovese. She was named after both Steve's father, an Italian tradition, and my mother. Her name also had a little something to do with my admiration for the late Jacqueline Kennedy. She was a miracle, from her tiny toes to her full head of dark hair. She was absolutely beautiful. Our sweet baby girl, Jacqueline, made me feel like our family was complete. Every dream I ever had, had come true. She was the perfect gift to our perfect little family.

After Jacqueline was born, my mother spent several weeks with us. She was such a great help. She cooked, she cleaned, and she did laundry, so all I had to do was concentrate on taking care of my sweet little Jacqueline. My mother enjoyed spending time with us, no matter what she was doing. In her new role as grandmother, she decided she wanted to be called Honey Gram. Well the Gram part did not stick, but the Honey definitely did. She totally embraced her new name and her new role in life, and she was also going to live up to that name, being sweet as honey. She loved being Jacqueline's Honey more than anything in the world.

I had thought Steve was protective only of me—until Jacqueline was born. She was his little princess. Steve made sure she had the best of everything. He researched the safety on every baby bed and high chair in the tri-state area. He made sure every electrical outlet had safety covers before Jacqueline could even roll over or sit up. Steve treated Jacqueline like she was a porcelain doll he had to protect at all cost.

My modeling career was on hold for a while so that I could be home with Jacqueline. I didn't mind at all, because I loved my new role as a mother.

Having a baby didn't stop Steve and me from enjoying our nights out, but now we were a party of three. I dressed Jacqueline up in her beautiful smocked dresses and Texas-size bow, and we took her out with us wherever we went. Steve loved doing this and showing her off. She was always the best baby, content to sit in her highchair for hours, perfectly entertained by almost anything.

Having Jacqueline was like having my own little playmate. We made many trips into the city, went shopping and to museums and parks, and visited friends during the day. But now that I had a baby, it wasn't as convenient or as easy for me to hop on a flight to Dallas. Therefore, my mother would fly back and forth to New Jersey to spend time with us. Honey could hardly stand being away from us.

When Jacqueline was five months old, it was finally time to move into our new home. For the past year and a half, I'd been overseeing every detail. It was my own little castle in New Jersey, a beautiful and unique brick home at the end of a heavily wooded lot. The house had gothic-shaped windows, hand-distressed wood columns, breathtaking murals, and wrought iron gates and chandeliers. We had planned every detail of it. Steve and I were both so proud of our beautiful home that he'd worked so hard for.

Christmas 2000 had arrived, and we were just settling in. Steve wanted nothing more than to have a Christmas party at our new home to celebrate the season. The house wasn't completely finished, and I really wanted to wait until it was decorated before we had anyone over. The thought of having a party so quickly was definitely out of my comfort zone. Steve insisted and jokingly said that no one cared if my monogram towels hadn't come in yet for the bathroom. He was ready to enjoy our beautiful new home. Stepping out of my comfort zone was well worth it, because we had an unbelievable evening. It was a Christmas I'll never forget.

When Jacqueline was nearly seven months old, my agent and my clients were ready for me to get back to work. I was ready also, but I was having a hard time leaving my sweet baby girl. She had become my world, and it was so hard to trust anyone to take care of her. I was lucky that Steve's mom, Vera, was right down the street and able to watch Jacqueline during the day while I worked. But it wasn't the same as having my mother there. I desperately wished my mother lived nearby.

Steve was a great dad and provided for his family well. He loved to play with Jacqueline when he got home from work, taking her for strolls around the neighborhood, carrying her around on his shoulders, playing peekaboo with her, and tucking his little princess into bed at night. But it was difficult for him at times to let go of his independent lifestyle he was accustomed to. He'd been a bachelor for over thirty-five years; he was used to being on his own schedule and being able to do what he wanted, when he wanted. For me, this had never been a problem, but now that we had Jacqueline, my life was different. I wasn't able to jump on a plane to Texas every time I would start to feel homesick.

It had never bothered me before that Steve went out with his buddies or would entertain late nights after work. But now it was starting to get in my head. A seed of resentment had started to take root in my mind. Once again I was homesick, and I was also starting to deal with depression. It was an extremely cold winter, I was hardly working, and Jacqueline and I were stuck in the house. There were so many hours in the day when we were alone. Isolated and alone with my thoughts.

Sometimes Steve had to entertain on weeknights. There were days I barely saw him because he would have to leave for work so early and got home so late. I loved him more than anything, but I was starting to resent his staying out late and being able to do what he wanted.

Over the past couple of years, my life had changed dramatically. I'd given up my life in Texas to be with him. I just wanted to see that his life was changing as well. He was working so hard to give me everything he thought I wanted and would make me happy, but all I wanted was for him to spend more time with us. I was feeling lonelier than ever as I sat day after day in the beautiful home he'd built for us.

Now that we'd built our dream home in New Jersey, I realized my dream of moving back to Texas was not going to happen. This was devastating for me to think about. And my mom realized it too. I spent many hours during the day talking to her on the phone while Jacqueline napped. I began to vent to her. She often reminded me that Steve had promised he would move us to Texas once we had children. But I knew it wasn't happening.

My mom was having a really hard time being away from Jacqueline, and I knew she wanted to help me anyway she could. She started coming to visit often and staying for weeks at a time. I loved having her there, and it helped ease my loneliness, but this didn't always make Steve happy. The more time she spent in New Jersey, the more time Steve spent finding other things to do besides being at home. The whole situation was causing tremendous stress on our marriage.

Steve was also feeling a heavy load on his shoulders. He'd saved money his whole life. He wasn't used to spending so much money so quickly, as he had with building and furnishing our new house, and with his expanding family—not to mention a mother-in-law who was basically living with us. He was stressed, and I was depressed. It was a bad combination.

Having Jacqueline made me realize how much I missed being surrounded by my family. I'd let small amounts of loneliness, resentment, and bitterness begin to fester in my heart. Steve began to notice that this feeling wasn't going away, but was beginning to intensify. He wished my mother would spend less time with us in New Jersey, thinking that this would give me more of an opportunity to make his home my home.

Steve wanted more of me, but so did my mother. I was allowing myself to be pulled in two different directions.

I needed to get these negative thoughts out of my head. They'd started off small but would soon consume my every thought. I wasn't fully embracing my wonderful new life God had so blessed me with. I was looking back on the past, wishing I was still there. I wanted it all! I wanted my precious little family and beautiful home, but I also wanted somehow for all of us to be in Texas.

The summer of 2001 was time for our annual Pointer family vacation to Destin, Florida. I was excited yet nervous about our time with my family. This trip created even more friction that had been growing for months between my mother and Steve— two very strong personalities who felt they were at odds in competition for Jacqueline and me.

It all finally exploded. Words were spoken between them, feelings were hurt, and I was stuck right in the middle.

I'd never really learned how to deal with conflict, so immediately after the big blowup between my mother and Steve, I decided not to deal with it. I acted like nothing had happened and prayed it would all just go away. I left the condo to go into town to do a little shopping. I stumbled upon a place called the Magnolia House. Walking in felt comforting and peaceful, with the smell of burning candles and beautiful music playing softly in the background. I wished I could stay in that happy place forever and not have to deal with what was going on back at the condo.

I looked around the adorable shop and made a small purchase, continuing to pretend like my life wasn't falling apart. The woman at the counter struck up a conversation with me. She had such a kind demeanor, and you could tell she was so genuine. Somehow, it was as if she knew I was going through inner turmoil, because she said she had something she wanted to give me. She handed me a notecard with a poem written on it. I thanked her, and later, as I got into my car, I read.

> Our lives are on a journey, and we may not pass this
> way again.
> So hold on to the moment, and do all that you can.
> For though grace is sufficient for the day,
> moments, like eagles, fly away.
> *(by Nancy Veldman)*

It was as if God had sent an angel to give me a gift, a gift that opened my eyes. At that very moment, I knew things in my life had to change.

This was my season to be with my husband. I had to stop living in the past. I had to stop feeling sorry for myself, wishing my life away, always wanting to be back in Texas. I needed to make the most of every moment of every day, because moments fly away! I would never have this time back, and I was going to do all I could to make things right in our marriage.

I still have that notecard framed on my nightstand, as a reminder to seize every moment.

When Steve and I returned home from the Florida trip, we both knew something had happened over the last few months that had put our marriage on a dangerous edge where neither of us wanted to be. The past year had brought so many changes for both of us. We talked like we never had before about the struggles that had been going on the last couple of months in our marriage. I knew that I'd experienced inner turmoil and depression from being away from my family that I couldn't seem to shake. I also knew that I'd always seemed to continually put my mother first. Steve struggled with my mother visiting so much and with feeling like he was always second to her.

It had been five years since we were married, and I wondered if I'd really ever given 100 percent of myself to my new life in New Jersey. I'd spent years looking back and wishing I was in Texas. I needed to live in the moment. I needed to put my husband first. I'd truly never done that. Now it was time.

I loved Steve and I loved my mother, but I knew I had to do what was right: put Steve first.

We decided that summer that we would seek the guidance of a marriage counselor to help us work through our struggles. We were never going to give up on our family. We knew that our love was strong and could break through any barriers. We saw no shame in seeking help.

It was the best decision we'd ever made. After we began seeing a Christian counselor, it made me realize that years before I'd left a large part of my heart in Texas. But now my family was Steve and Jacqueline, and my heart had to be wherever they were. I had to finally come to terms with the fact that Steve loved New Jersey just as much as I loved Texas, and New York was where he needed to be for his profession.

I'd lost myself somewhere along the path, not realizing how blessed I was and not being content with my life. I needed to get my priorities straight and turn back to Christ. He'd never left me. I had just strayed from Him, and He was pulling me back in. I needed to be back in Bible study and spending more time in God's Word. I knew that if I drew near to Christ, He would draw near to me. Most importantly, I knew I needed to truly begin to pray for my marriage that the enemy was trying to devour.

Steve and I immediately started attending church on a regular basis, I got involved in a Bible study group, and Jacqueline and I started having playdates. I didn't travel to Texas on weekends, but stayed at home with my family. I started praying for my marriage like I never had before. The heavy weight of loneliness, resentment, and bitterness I'd felt was lifted. Once I didn't call Texas my home, I could make a home in New Jersey.

I was so ready to be the best wife I could possibly be. We were given a fresh start, and all because God decided to speak to me through a poem.

In August 2001, one of my childhood best friends was getting married in Las Vegas. Steve and I were flying to Vegas for the weekend. It reminded us both of our own special love. We had such a great weekend, and we were even asked several times if we were on our honeymoon. We just loved being together. Jacqueline spent that weekend with my family in Dallas, and I was flying there to pick her up on my way back to New Jersey. Steve was leaving Las Vegas on an earlier flight to return to New Jersey.

Early that morning, I walked him to the door of our hotel room, I kissed him goodbye and watched him walk away down the long hallway. I had a strange sense of complete love for this man. Not that I didn't have complete love for him before, but this feeling was deeper. We'd gotten through a difficult time in our marriage and come out on the other side. Yes, our marriage had growing pains, but now it was stronger than ever before. Our whole marriage we'd spent weekends walking away from each other, both selfishly doing our own thing. But this time I noticed that seeing him walk away made me sad in a deep place in my heart. I already missed him, and he wasn't even gone.

I ran down the long hall just to give him one more kiss.

As I walked back into my hotel room, I knew I'd finally conquered my inner ache to be in Texas. I couldn't wait to be back home so I could be with Steve. Things had changed for me in my heart and in my mind. Home was wherever Steve was!

CHAPTER 6

Do not boast about tomorrow,
for you do not know what a day may bring.

PROVERBS 27:1 NIV

Going into the fall of 2001, Steve and I found ourselves excited about life. Our relationship was stronger than ever, and I was ecstatic about my world and everything in it. It was my favorite time of year in New Jersey as the leaves were changing into beautiful bright colors, the air had a brisk feel, and life was surreal once again.

Jacqueline was sixteen months old, and she was a living doll, walking and talking up a storm. Steve often boasted, as any good dad should, about how advanced his daughter was.

I was back to steady work and had gotten several new modeling accounts. One was with Neiman Marcus in Westchester County in Upstate New York. I especially loved working for Neiman's because of the 30 percent discount I received on the days I worked. Steve would often say, "I'll pay you *not* to work for Neiman's, because I think we're losing money on this one. Shelly René, do you know what deficit is?" I was definitely spending more money than I was making on this particular job and enjoying every minute of it. I was just taking advantage of the perks. Steve of course loved that I was working and that he had back the Shelly René he knew and loved.

My mother hadn't been up to New Jersey for quite some time because she was giving Steve and I personal space. I know it was very difficult for her not being able to spend weeks at a time with Jacqueline and me, but she knew it was for the best. She'd been eagerly waiting for us to come to Texas on September 8 for my brother Price's twenty-first birthday. It had been way too long, and she was ready to spend lots of time with us, especially with Jacqueline. And she knew she would be returning to New Jersey with us on Monday to babysit Jacqueline for the week while I worked for Neiman's. She hadn't spent much time with Steve since the big blow-up in Florida and was a bit apprehensive. She decided to ask her best friend of thirty years, Dale Nichols (better known as Big Mama) to join her in New Jersey for the week. Big Mama had visited New Jersey with Honey several times, but she had a family of her own and wasn't sure she would be able to pick up and leave. Honey was very persuasive and talked her into it. Big Mama had always been like a second mother to me, and I was very excited she was going to be able to make the trip on such short notice. This was also going to be a great comfort to Honey, knowing she had Big Mama to hang out with during the week while Steve and I worked. It all seemed to work out perfectly.

A couple of days before our planned trip to Dallas, Steve wasn't feeling well and considered staying home for the weekend. I ended up convincing him to make the trip, telling him he would feel better by Friday. I knew it was going to be a fun weekend, and I didn't want to spend it without him.

Steve, Jacqueline, and I all made the trip to Dallas on September 7, 2001. The next day, we celebrated my brother's birthday at my parents' house in Rowlett, Texas. All of Price's friends and our family came together for his big celebration. My brother was excited we were there, especially Steve. Price and Steve had always been close. Steve was almost fifteen years older and Price really looked up to him in many ways. Steve was like a big brother to Price, who was the little brother Steve never had.

Steve spent time with Price teaching him the ropes. They always seemed to have tons of fun together, often getting into mischief. Even though Steve was a Christian, he was no saint, nor was Price. They spent many nights asking for forgiveness instead of permission. That night, Steve did a great job playing the big brother role to all of Price's friends, always making sure everyone was having a good time. He was great at entertaining, and this night was no exception. I glanced over at him several times that evening, realizing how blessed I was to have this incredible man in my life.

After an unforgettable weekend in Dallas, Steve returned home on Sunday, September 9, so he could be ready for work the next morning. Jacqueline and I had decided to stay in Texas for an extra night. That way we could have a little bonus time to spend with my family.

On Monday afternoon September 10, Jacqueline, Honey, Big Mama and I headed to DFW airport, boarded our flight, and headed to New Jersey. They were so excited to spend the week with us. We talked about our plans and all the new things I couldn't wait to show them. It had been months since their last visit, and I was excited they were coming home with me. They were also going to be in town for my twenty-eighth birthday on September 16.

Having them in our house again made me ecstatic. I decided to call in pizza for dinner, as Steve helped Honey and Big Mama get their things settled in their guest rooms upstairs. He was happy to have "his girls" (Jacqueline and me) home, and I was happy to be home. I was so relieved that everybody was getting along and the burden of being pulled in so many different directions had been lifted.

It had been a long day traveling for my baby girl. It was time for her to be put down for the night. I felt like I needed to stock up on groceries because I knew it was going to be a busy week, and I might not have time to go. There was also a brand-new Texas-size grocery store that had just opened up not far away, and I could hardly wait for Honey and Big Mama to check it out. I knew that Honey was always up for a little night shopping. I would normally have gone to bed with Steve at this time, a habit we started early on in our marriage, but going to the grocery store seem to be a priority.

With Steve and Jacqueline settled for the night, we were off to the supersized grocery store. We talked and laughed like a bunch of teenagers as we went down every aisle, not wanting to miss a thing. By the time we returned home with a car full of groceries, Jacqueline and Steve had been fast asleep for hours.

Looking back, it's unbelievable to me to think how God had made a way to bring these two godly women to New Jersey to be with us for what was about to become the most devastating journey of our lives.

I crawled into bed with Steve and cuddled up next to him. I wanted so badly to wake him up and tell him how excited I was about the awesome new grocery store, but there would always be tomorrow. I closed my eyes and went to sleep, happy and content with my life and the week ahead.

CHAPTER 7

Do not be far from me,
for trouble is near
and there is no one to help.

PSALM 22:11 NIV

T he next morning, Tuesday, September 11, 2001, was a day no one could have ever imagined happening, much less being thrust into.

As always, Steve woke up early. He left Jacqueline and me sleeping while he got ready for work. Every morning he went in to check on Jacqueline and give his little princess a kiss. That morning, I felt Steve gently kiss me. He then reached over and turned the ringer off on the phone that was on the nightstand beside the bed. He was always considerate, not wanting anyone to wake me before Jacqueline did. And she always had a way of letting us know when she was ready to start her day. She wasn't an early riser, which was a blessing, because everyone knew I required more sleep than most.

That morning, he got into his car and headed to the train station. Honey and Big Mama both heard him leaving. For some reason, in two separate guest rooms on opposite ends of our house, instinctively both of them looked out their window and saw Steve driving away. As Big Mama looked out, she also noticed that it was going to be an exceptionally beautiful sunny day.

It was still very early, and they both crawled back into bed.

Every day when Steve reached his office, he phoned his father, and they would talk briefly before his work day began. This day was no different. He spoke to his father just hours before unimaginable horror would unfold.

Hours later on this clear September day, I was still fast asleep. The phone began to ring, and ring, and ring—but I never heard a sound, since the phone by my nightstand was turned off, and I couldn't hear the phone ringing from the nearby guest room. That sound had been muffled by the box fan I'd slept with since childhood.

Honey was finally awakened by the phone. It had rung repeatedly, then did so again a second time. By the third time, she got out of bed to answer it, realizing someone must have wanted to get hold of us. It was Mary Kay emphatically telling her to immediately wake me up and turn on the TV, because something had happened to Steve's building.

With concern, Honey quickly rushed into my room and switched on the lights. She told me Mary Kay had called and that something had happened to the World Trade Center.

I jumped out of bed and turned on the TV. Still groggy, with my eyes barely open, I stared at the TV. The North Tower where Steve worked on the 104th floor, had bright orange flames coming out of the building. A cloud of black smoke billowed around the tower and filled the air. This couldn't be real; it was something you would see in the movies, not real life.

What was going on? What happened? I'd just fallen to sleep in Steve's arm. I had no idea what opening my eyes on this day was going to hold for my family.

By this time, Honey and Big Mama were both in the master bedroom with me. I immediately tried to call Steve, but phone circuits were inundated with calls in our region, and I couldn't get through to him. I continued to dial his number over and over.

Then Honey remembered that the phone had been ringing that morning continuously. She thought Steve might have tried to call. I was immediately devastated to think I might had missed his call. My heart beat out of my chest as I quickly retrieved my voicemail.

What I heard was a frantic call from Steve with terror in his voice. I'd never heard him like this before. He was yelling, begging me: "Shelly, pick up the phone, wake up! Pick up the phone! I think a plane just hit my building." It wasn't what he said that really struck me; it was the fear and desperation in his voice, mixed with the muffled sounds of chaos in the background—then silence.

I was so mad at myself. Why didn't I answer that call? Steve was so scared! He needed me, and I wasn't there for him. I continued trying to get in touch with Steve, with no success.

My eyes were glued to the TV. The media was speculating that a private plane had hit the North Tower. I sat in my bed motionless, staring at the familiar building wrapped in smoke and flames, wondering what was going on inside.

About this time, Jacqueline woke up. Big Mama went in to care for her and we all quickly made our way downstairs. Other people started calling me, trying to figure out if I'd heard from Steve. With every ring, I immediately answered the phone, praying I would hear Steve's voice. I desperately needed reassurance, to give me the comfort I didn't receive from his first call.

No one was panicking; we were just all in shock. Everyone, like the media, thought it was a crazy freak accident. We knew Steve had called, and we immediately assumed he was okay. He must at that moment be making his way out of the building. But I knew one thing for sure: he was terrified. I had heard it in his voice.

It had been less than twenty minutes, but felt like a lifetime waiting anxiously for Steve to call again. Firefighters and police had all been dispatched from all over the city and were heading into the North Tower, helping thousands get out of the building safely.

Mary Kay was the first to arrive at my house. We were gathered in the family room with all eyes on the North Tower, when the unthinkable happened. At 9:03, before our very eyes, we watched a large jet airplane come out of nowhere and plunge into the South Tower of the World Trade Center. It seemed as though this plane just disappeared into the side of the building, followed by a massive explosion and flames.

Everything changed at that very moment. I was living the worst nightmare I could ever have imagined. Paralyzed with fear, I realized this was no accident. We knew our country was under attack.

All I could think about was Steve getting out of that building. I wanted him home and knew he had to be on his way down. I began trying my best to figure out where the plane had hit the North Tower, from where the fire appeared to be located, but in 2001 we had no ability to pause the TV screen. I stood close to the TV and began to count windows starting from the top each time the TV camera focused on the North Tower. It was frustrating because the networks would shift to another image as I was trying my best to count, and I had to start over again each time the building was shown.

The news reports were stating that the North Tower had been hit somewhere around the eightieth or eighty-fifth floor (though it was actually higher—between the ninety-third and ninety-ninth). They also reported that both buildings were being evacuated. I remembered Steve telling me that after the 1993 bombing, it had taken him three hours to walk down from his office on the 104th floor. Again I thought, *He's in the stairway, making his way down once more. That's why I can't get in touch with him.*

My phone was constantly ringing. Everyone was trying to determine what was going on inside the towers and with our country.

Within a matter of minutes, the house was filled with friends and neighbors. We were scared, but we all continued to think that if anyone could get out of that building, it was going to be Steve. I remember thinking, *Things like this don't happen to me. They happen to other people.* Not me, not my husband—he was getting out of that building and coming home.

Reports soon came that another aircraft had hit the Pentagon. There were other reports and rumors of a plane heading toward Washington. The White House and U.S. Capitol building were being evacuated.

I was so anxious about what could possibly happen next. It was terrifying to think about.

In the midst of everything, all I could think about was Steve. I could only imagine how the stairways must have been filled with smoke. How much longer was it going to take him to get out?

What we saw on TV seemed so unreal. I didn't understand why they couldn't just send a helicopter to rescue the people who appeared in the upper-story windows of the towers, waving for someone to save them. We were shocked at what the media was saying about desperate people who faced a terrible choice of burning to death or jumping.

I was praying that I would hear from Steve soon. Hoping someone had seen him, or knew something—*anything.*

I hadn't moved from where I was standing. I wasn't about to. I kept praying for Steve's safety, continuing to tell myself, *He's a survivor.* He'd survived the terrorist attack in 1993, and he was going to get out of that building.

At 9:59, in complete disbelief, we watched the South Tower collapse.

Silent. Speechless. Devastated for the lives lost in that building. It was inconceivable to everyone that this gigantic tower could collapse and actually had.

I was in complete shock that this was all happening before our eyes. Terrified, I thought, *Thank God, that wasn't Steve's building.* I can't explain my inability to think of anything else except Steve. The more chaos that was going on all around me, the more I started to block out everything. Everything, except Steve.

It had been a little over an hour since Steve's building had been hit. I knew he must have been almost halfway down by now. The North Tower was still on fire and filling up with smoke, but at least it was still standing. I waited anxiously, as I thanked God for giving Steve more time to escape.

Watching the TV, we saw people covered in ash and soot, running through smoke-filled streets, covering their faces with whatever they could to avoid breathing in the smoke. I watched with desperation, wanting to see Steve there as well. I'd completely convinced myself that the people I was seeing on TV had escaped from the North Tower and were making their way home. Steve was going to be one of those people. He was going to have another story to tell about how he made it out of America's worst terrorist attack. I knew he would make it home—he would find a way out! He would never leave Jacqueline and me alone in this world.

Minutes seemed like hours as we all stood in front of the TV. Not even thirty minutes after the South Tower collapsed, I watched in disbelief as the North Tower crashed to the ground, collapsing into a pile of dust. In an instant, it was gone.

It was then that I, too, collapsed. My whole world came crashing down the moment the tower fell. I fell to the floor screaming, crying, calling out to God. Gasping for air as I cried uncontrollably. I screamed out loud to God: "*No! Not Steve!* NO, NOT STEVE!" I knew Steve had not had three hours to make it out of the building.

My mind was filled with racing thoughts. I cried and screamed out again to God to save Steve. "*O Lord, save Steve!*" If only one was saved, let it be Steve.

At this moment, something incredible happened, as I lay on the floor sobbing uncontrollably. Suddenly, as if God was calming the raging sea, I felt a comfort, a calming feeling. I felt that God had heard my prayers and answered them instantly. A complete peace that wasn't humanly understandable came over me, a peace and a comfort like I'd never known. I'd called out for

God to save Steve; I trusted Him, knowing He could. I knew it would have to be a miracle, but I believed in miracles.

This would be the first and almost the last time I would publicly collapse into tears and despair. I had an indescribable peace, and I had faith that could move a mountain. This was going to be my story: God was going to bring my husband home!

In this moment, I believed that the comfort and peace that came over me was God answering my prayers. Even though it seemed humanly impossible for anyone to survive the towers crumbling to the ground, I knew my God could do anything. The God I served was a God of miracles. Even the impossible.

I stopped crying, got up off the floor, and calmly began to wait for Steve's arrival home. I went upstairs to our bedroom to get dressed and put on make up, so that when Steve got home he would say to me once again, "Shelly René, you're a sight for sore eyes." And he would smile at me with his gigantic smile.

I went into the kitchen and began to cook dinner for Steve, including his favorite—strawberry bread. My heart's desire was for Steve to walk through the door to an unbelievable homecoming. The house would be filled with all his favorite people, and it was going to be a celebration. He'd made it out in 1993, and somehow, he'd found a way to make it out of this attack too.

I began carrying on with my day as usual, anticipating Steve's homecoming. I even asked Big Mama to go next door to borrow an extra pan to bake the strawberry bread in. When she went outside, she was frightened, because a huge fighter plane flew right over our house. No one knew what to expect next. Life seemed so uncertain, and everyone was terrified. But I continued to block out everything. I just kept telling myself that Steve was going to make it home to "his girls."

Mayor Rudy Giuliani ordered evacuation of lower Manhattan, and thousands of people made their way on foot across the Brooklyn Bridge. Rescue teams searched for survivors at the World Trade Center and the surrounding area. We began calling hospitals and gathering photos of Steve to take into the city to ask the people on the streets if anyone had seen him. Soon flyers and photos of missing loved ones were posted all over Manhattan. Everyone was looking for someone—husbands, wives, mothers, fathers, sons, daughters, and friends.

Although I still hadn't heard from Steve, there was no doubt in my mind that he was alive. But as the day went on, I wondered why he wasn't home yet. I started to think that maybe he had a head injury and couldn't remember his name—that's why he hadn't called home. But I never thought for one second that he wasn't coming home. I thought maybe he was in one of the makeshift hospitals in Manhattan, and when he was able to, he would call. Maybe he was stuck in the rubble and waiting to be rescued. I just knew he was coming home, and Jacqueline and I were going to be there waiting for him when he walked through the door.

Throughout the long day, Honey and Big Mama took care of Jacqueline and helped everyone gather any information they could to help find Steve. While glancing at the TV and the terror in New York City, not being able to fully comprehend what we were living through.

God had already placed me in a protective cocoon. I already knew that His hands were on me. Just the sheer fact that He had allowed my mother and Big Mama to be with me in New Jersey during the most horrific day of my life was simply God's grace. He allowed them to be there to take care of me, take care of Jacqueline, and support each other. If we hadn't flown to New Jersey on September 10, just the night before, I would have been stuck in Dallas and unable to make it home, since all air traffic in the United States had been grounded. God had made a way for us all to be there together.

Everyone seemed glued to the TV, but I never watched it for long. I couldn't stand to listen to what the media was saying. I knew that the negativity and horror they reported—with thousands dead—would fill my mind. I needed to stay strong in my faith. I so strongly believed that the Lord was going to bring Steve home; I didn't want to hear anything about anyone in the towers not being able to make it out in time. I felt like God had told me something different from what the world believed to be true.

A little after 8:00 p.m., President George W. Bush addressed the country and quoted Psalm 23: "Yea, though I walk through the valley of the shadow of death, I will fear no evil: for thou art with me; thy rod and thy staff, they comfort me" (KJV). God had comforted me with a peace I couldn't explain.

This had been the longest day of my life. I was physically exhausted. Big Mama put Jacqueline in her crib for the night. It was hard to believe that I didn't want the worst day of my life to be over, but I didn't. I longed for Steve to walk through the door. I couldn't even think about going to bed without knowing he was safe, but somehow in my heart I knew he was.

But there was also a part of me that just wanted to go to sleep, so that when I woke up, Steve would be there lying at my side. I wanted his strong arms wrapped around me, and his voice telling me everything was going to be okay.

I laid in my bed for hour just praying for him to walk through the door.

The emptiness in my bed was unnerving. Honey and Big Mama crawled in my big empty bed with me, then decided to give me a sleeping pill. They had no idea what tomorrow was going to bring, and they knew I needed to rest. Honey even joked about Steve walking in and seeing all of us all cuddled up in his bed. I wanted so badly for that to happen.

We all prayed together, praying for our nation and for Steve's safety, knowing that the prayers were the only thing that was keeping us going. We had to have hope—and we did.

My mom was always dressing me up and taking pictures

Playing in our family room with my little brother Price

Some of my first modeling test shots

Modeling in the early 90s

Miss Dallas 1992
Christmas tree lighting
at Scottish Rite Hospital
with Luke
Dallas, Texas

1992 Miss Texas USA Pageant held
in Corpus Christi, Texas
Miss East Texas

First official date with Steve at the Old Warsaw, Dallas, Texas

Mr. and Mrs. Steven Gregory Genovese
Crescent Court Hotel, Dallas, Texas
November 18, 1997

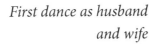

First dance as husband and wife

STEVE'S BABY GIRL

Proud Daddy
Jacqueline's first day home from the hospital

Daddy's home from work and
Jacqueline's ready to play

Easter 2001

Trip to the Bronx Zoo
Summer 2001

FAMILY TIME

Karaoke fun at my parents house

Jacqueline's first birthday celebrated in Connecticut

Steve and his girls

Jacqueline would often say her Daddy was "up" and point to heaven

Trip to the Peabody Hotel in Tennessee with Honey and Jacqueline to watch the ducks walk through the hotel lobby

Mom, Dad, Price, and I playing dress up with Jacqueline

*Jacqueline was very excited
when Heath gave her a
precious ring and asked if he
could marry her mom*

*Engaged to Heath
and loving my life*

*Just Married
True Texas style departure
from The Mansion
on Turtle Creek
November 18, 2005*

MY HOPE

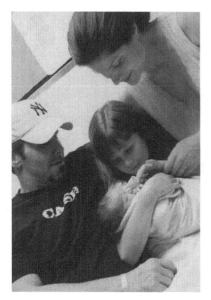

Welcoming Cash Calhoun into the family

My family, my world

God, your God, will restore everything you lost;
he'll have compassion on you; he'll come back
and pick up the pieces from all the places
where you were shattered.

DEUTERONOMY 30:3 MESSAGE

CHAPTER 8

And the peace of God,

which surpasses all understanding,

will guard your hearts and minds

in Christ Jesus.

PHILIPPIANS 4:7 ESV

Before opening my eyes the next morning, September 12, I prayed everything had all just been a horrible nightmare. Opening them, I realized I was actually living the nightmare.

Steve was still missing. His army of friends were already heading into the city to look for him. They joined the masses of people looking for their loved ones in Manhattan, asking anyone and everyone if they'd seen or heard anything about where Steve might be. Countless hours had been spent on the computer, printing flyers with Steve's photos and our contact information.

I stayed home, anxiously waiting by the phone for his call. We all just wanted Steve to be found, but we knew at this point he had to be injured or we would have heard from him by now. We desperately needed to find out where he was so we could go to him.

Friends and neighbors were offering support in every way, praying for us, taking care of Jacqueline, or helping Honey feed the crowds who were working tirelessly to help find Steve. I found myself increasingly overwhelmed. I just needed to be by myself and with God.

I often sat on the floor in the walk-in closet of our master bedroom. It had a large window that the sun would stream through. I shut myself off from the world. I needed to feel close to Steve. I would sit on the floor, holding his shirts close to my face, just to smell the scent of his cologne. It made me feel safe, secure, like he was with me.

I looked outside at the beautiful sky and prayed, knowing God could answer my prayer, and wondering why He hadn't. I continued to think about the message Steve had left me. I was so devastated by the fact that I hadn't answered the phone. I listened to the message over and over, until it began to haunt me. I eventually decided to erase it. I never wanted anyone to have to hear what I heard. Only a few people ever heard this message.

In the days that followed, I found myself still dazed. I was just walking around in survival mode, trying to make it through each day. I showed very little emotion. I'd completely stopped watching TV. I couldn't handle watching the buildings crumble to the ground over and over, or to see the empty New York skyline where only days before the Twin Towers stood.

I wouldn't speak to anyone who didn't believe that Steve could have made it out of the building alive. I wasn't listening to what the world was saying, because my hope was not in the world, but in Jesus.

Honey and Big Mama were saints. They took care of everything. They would come into my closet to check on me, to make sure that I was eating, or to let me know that someone had arrived that I needed to see. I knew everything was being taken care of, including my precious Jacqueline. I was able to survive only by holding on to God's promises. I knew that God promised to never leave me nor forsake me. I felt His presence with me at all times. He never left my side. I just couldn't handle being around so many people. I knew they were there for me, but all I needed was to be alone with God. It was the only thing that was getting me through. He was the only hope I had.

At the end of each day, Steve's friends would return to the house with no sign of him. They were emotionally drained by what they'd seen and running out of hope.

On Thursday evening, September 13, Steve's brother, JJ, was on *Larry King Live*. I saw the pain in his face as he held up a photo of his only sibling and best friend, and pleaded for anyone with information to help. At this point, everyone knew that it would have to be a miracle for Steve to be alive.

Ground Zero had gone from a rescue mission to a mission of recovering bodies. They hadn't found anyone alive in the rubble since the early morning on September 12. Thousands of volunteers searched the debris where the towers once stood. It was like a war zone, and thousands had perished. Everyone was desperate to find their loved ones. Even if it was just to get closure.

As the days passed, Steve's friends made their way out to his garage, where they could talk openly about the reality of Steve not being able to make it out of the building. They continued to protect me by being optimistic, all the while knowing that no one in the North Tower would have been able to survive if they were above the floors where the plane had struck.

But I would have nothing of that. Inside the house, the television wasn't on, and no newspapers were in sight. I would listen only to the little voice inside my heart and head that quietly calmed me. In my heart, I knew everything was going to be all right. I listened to my praise music each day and retreated often to my closet. I continued to get dressed each day, making sure I was ready for Steve's homecoming.

One night, I asked our friends and neighbors to come together to pray for Steve and for the nation. As we stood outside on our back deck making a large circle, my heart began to ache. I looked around to see our many friends and neighbors who I'd never shared my faith in Jesus with. They had no idea with whom I placed my hope. Sure, they knew I was a Christian girl from Texas, and they knew they couldn't use the Lord's name in vain around me. But did they understand who my God was? What He was capable of! Where I was getting my strength?

These past years I'd never stopped believing in Christ nor trusting Him—but had I shared my faith with my friends and neighbors? Was I really different from anyone else? Everything in my life had been wonderful, a fairy tale. I had a blessed life— but was I living it for Christ? Or had I been coasting through life with no real purpose?

Here I was in the midst of my darkest days; I needed Christ now more than ever, and *He* was there for me!

I was surrounded by people I loved and who loved my family. As I stood there, I didn't feel sorry for myself. I didn't feel sorry for Jacqueline. I just felt intense guilt that I'd never shared the love of Jesus with all the people who had been placed in my life.

Before I prayed, I apologized. I told them how important Jesus Christ was in my life and how important He was in Steve's life. I'd never strayed from my faith in Christ, but I'd taken it for granted that I was bought by the blood of Christ and set apart for God's purpose. I knew nothing could ever strip me from His hands.

In that instant, I was reminded of my purpose in this world. I don't even know what I prayed that night, but I do know that I asked for forgiveness from God and from the people He'd placed in my life.

On Friday, September 14, my dad and brother arrived in New Jersey. All flights had been grounded in the United States immediately after the attacks, and this was the first flight they were able to get on. It had been so difficult for them to not be able to be there with us during this unfathomable time.

Steve's brother, JJ, and one of Steve's closest friends went to the airport to pick up my dad and brother. I hadn't left my house, still awaiting Steve's arrival home. I had a tremendous faith and hope that he was coming home, but I was desperately longing to see his face. Everyone else, however, had by this point come to the painful realization that Steve had not made it out. I could hear everyone whispering, and they would often walk outside so they could talk. Everyone was definitely starting to think I was going a little crazy.

Honey and Big Mama knew that it was God protecting me. They, too, believed God could do the impossible. But reality was looking grim. They had to be so strong during the day and hold everything in as they continued to protect me, but at night they would often go into their rooms to cry and pray together, praying that God would soon reveal the truth.

I needed to get out of the house. I hadn't seen the outside world in almost a week. I asked Honey and Big Mama to take me out for a drive, to get some fresh air. We left the house like normal, but there was nothing normal about my next request—to stop and shop at TJ Maxx.

I remember walking into the store. It was a very strange feeling to be outside my house, away from my comfort zone. I felt like I was a walking zombie. I was walking, talking, but it was like I wasn't really there. It felt surreal, as if I was in a haze. It felt like I'd taken several Benadryl, or was heavily sedated.

I walked around the store and ended up in the men's section. I picked out several shirts for Steve. As I held them up, I asked my mom, "Do you think Steve would like these shirts?" Maybe it was the look on her face; suddenly nausea swept my entire body. I had to leave immediately! I went back home to my safe spot, the closet. I could not handle reality! Again, all I could do was pray and listen to my praise music to remain in the reality I so desperately wanted.

September 16 was my birthday, and Honey and Big Mama tried to make it as special for me as possible, throwing me a little get-together at the house. I just knew in my heart of hearts that this was going to be the day Steve walked in through the door. It was going to be the best birthday present I could ever imagine. Oh, the story it would be!

It was starting to be painful for everyone to watch me. Steve's closest friends came together, as they had every day since the attacks, and they decided it was time that I should be told the truth—that Steve was not coming home.

A close friend of Steve's, Tony, brought me a beautiful bouquet of roses. He said, "Steve would have wanted you to have them." Tony had been going through his own mental torture since September 11. He worked for Cantor Fitzgerald as well, but wasn't at work on the day of the attack. He'd been in Denver for the start of the 2001 NFL Monday night football season, with the Denver Broncos taking on the New York Giants. I secretly wished that Steve had been a Giants fan, so he could have safely been in Denver with Tony.

Tony was so strong, but he had to be in such pain, facing a great deal of survivor's guilt. The weight of losing hundreds of his closest friends and colleagues must have been overwhelming.

We sat in my kitchen privately, as he gently tried to explain to me that no one had been recovered from Ground Zero in days, and that I had to try to accept the reality that Steve had not made it out. Tony told me that no one in the building from the North Tower above the ninety-first floor had survived the attack. He was sorry that he had to tell me this. He said he wished Steve had joined him on his trip to Denver.

I looked at him, and I listened to every word that came out of his mouth—but I didn't believe it. He was wrong. Steve was coming home, I knew it! My heart broke for Tony and for the pain he must have been going through. I also knew how much Tony meant to Steve. I thanked him for the beautiful flowers, and I assured him that Steve was strong and would come out of this alive. I walked away from Tony still completely assured that Steve was coming home. I had to believe it.

On Sunday, September 17, I woke up angry. I was ready for this nightmare to be over! I wanted my family back together. I wanted my husband home! How could everyone lose faith in Steve being found alive? I just could not lose that hope! It was all I had. I could not and I would not accept it.

I was angry at everyone. I knew that God could do great miracles; I never once doubted it. He'd given me an inner peace, and this had to mean that Steve was coming home. But why was he not home? Where was my husband?

This day meant nothing more to me than just another day without seeing my precious Steve's face. Everyone desperately wanted to help me, but it was heart-wrenching for them to watch me. They needed to grieve the loss of Steve and weren't able to do this around me or in our house.

Later that night, after Jacqueline was in bed, Honey and Big Mama and I left the house for the second time. Just the day before, we'd heard that an article had been written about Steve. Supposedly the story was on the cover of our township newspaper. We knew very little about this article. I wanted to see it for myself.

We drove to the closest newsstand. As I got out of the car and approached the newsstand, I could see a large photo of Steve with this headline: "Husband, father, friend, not coming home."

It all swept over me at once.

It was in this moment, from seeing the newspaper with those words in bold print, that I realized with certainty that Steve wasn't coming home. It stared me in the face. It was reality. It was the conclusion that everyone else I knew had made days earlier, but I had refused to hear of it. Now I knew it to be true.

As I crawled into the back seat of the car, I began to read the article out loud. With tears streaming down my face, I let everything out that I'd been holding back for almost a week. My heart was broken, physically pained. I sobbed in the car uncontrollably, with Honey and Big Mama by my side. I sobbed for what seemed to be hours, until I simply ran out of tears.

Steve's adventurous, wonderful, spirit-filled life had ended. My life would never be the same. All our hopes, all our dreams— vanished in an instant. I felt completely hopeless.

Everything I was feeling, all my intense pain and despair, was nothing compared to the pain I felt for my precious Jacqueline. How was I going to tell her? She was too young to understand that her daddy wasn't coming home. I thought about her running to the back door at five o'clock each night, calling out for her daddy, and him not being there for her. My mind raced as I thought about her future, to all the things Steve was going to miss: having her crawl up into his lap and putting her head on his shoulders, tickling her, seeing her off on her first day of school, and walking her down the aisle on her wedding day. She was only sixteen months old and would never truly know him. She would never understand the depths of his love for her. The pain that I felt over this was unbearable.

How was I going to do this on my own? I knew I wasn't strong enough. But I knew who was. Once again, I felt the presence of my Almighty God wrapping His arms around me, comforting me, and holding me. Scripture that I hadn't heard in years filled my heart and my mind—God's promises! He promised that He would be the father to the fatherless (Psalm 68:5), that He would never leave me nor forsake me (Deuteronomy 31:6); that when I am weak, then I am strong (2 Corinthians 12:10). In my hopeless despair, He let me know that His plan for my life would not be one of destruction but of hope: "'For I know the plans I have for you,' says the LORD. 'They are plans for good and not for disaster, to give you a future and a hope'" (Jeremiah 29:11NLT).

At that moment, God planted a seed of hope within me. God once again had given me a strength that was humanly impossible and the peace that surpasses all understanding—peace that comes only from knowing Christ. I knew that if I didn't cling tightly to God's Word and His promises, I would never be able to get out of bed again. I had to be strong for Jacqueline. She'd lost her father; I didn't want her to lose her mother too.

I couldn't fathom a day without Steve, much less a future. But I knew that God was going to take care of us.

I know the peace and comfort that I so strongly felt in that moment when the North Tower fell was the peace and reassurance that Steve had met his Lord and Savior. As the tower crumbled to the ground, I called out to God to save Steve—and He did. God had answered my prayers that day, though not in the way in which I wanted.

God had saved Steve years before, the moment he asked Jesus to be his Lord and Savior. Now, Steve was truly home! Not his earthly home, but his eternal home.

CHAPTER 9

I am the resurrection and the life.

Anyone who believes in me will live, even after dying

JOHN 11:25 NLT

'd finally come to the realization that Steve's life here on earth was over. I knew my life would be forever altered. And I began to see the suffering and loss that filled our country. I realized my eyes had been closed to the devastation in which I was living.

Since the morning of September 11, the first time I laid my eyes on the powerful tower blazing with smoke and fire, my mind had been able to think only of Steve. I never once thought about the thousands of others suffering, fighting for their lives inside those buildings. It was all I could handle just to think about my own husband. My eyes were now open, and I could see pain and grief all around me.

The days and weeks ahead would be difficult. I don't really remember doing much of anything except crying and praying. Once again in our closet, I felt Steve's presence. I would close my eyes as I held his shirts tightly against me and pretended that he was there with me. To this day, I still have his pillowcase that he slept on the night before 9/11. I tucked it away in a ziplock bag, never to be washed.

I prayed each day. Honestly, my prayers most days weren't even prayers; I was just saying God's name over and over. Calling out to Him to help me. I was so lost, so weak, I didn't even know what to pray. But God knew my heart. He knew I was depending on Him to get us through. I know that I had strength to endure each new day only because of the prayers of thousands of people around the world who were lifting us up, and because of the Holy Spirit Himself interceding for us: "In the same way, the Spirit helps us in our weakness. We do not know what we ought to pray for, but the Spirit himself intercedes for us through wordless groans" (Romans 8:26 NIV).

Every morning, I had to choose to get out of bed. I didn't always want to, but I would hear Jacqueline's sweet voice and was faced with a choice. I chose to be the best mother I could possibly be at the time.

I felt so extremely blessed to have Jacqueline. She made my life worth living. She was a little part of Steve that he'd left behind. She was his gift to me! For my precious Jacqueline, our sixteen-month-old daughter, life would now be so different from what we'd planned for her. I wondered how I was going to raise her without her daddy.

My family and friends never left my side, and I am forever grateful for them. My dad spent his days in New Jersey pulling Jacqueline up and down the streets of our neighborhood in her little red wagon. He loved being with her and was great at keeping her entertained. It was good for both of them to be together during this time.

My brother was dealing with his pain much differently, spending time with Steve's friends at the local pub. They always ended up back at my house in Steve's garage, where they all felt the closest to him.

Thousands of volunteers continued to work countless hours at Ground Zero, digging through the rubble trying to find the victims' bodies so they could be identified. I wasn't even sure if I wanted Steve to be found. This would mean closure, and closure was permanent.

In Manhattan, there was a makeshift relief hub set up for the victims' families at Chelsea Pier. Inside the large building, there was information about different charities and how they could help assist the victims' families. Honey and I had to make a trip into New York City to work with legal officials, and we provided them with Steve's hairbrush and his toothbrush for DNA purposes. This was my first trip into the city since the attacks. I hadn't been watching TV like most of America, and I was in shock at what I saw. Seeing the destruction and loss was like going into a war zone. It was very different from being in New Jersey, only forty miles away.

I saw the pain and heaviness of the brokenhearted. There was dust, paper, and debris everywhere. Photographs of innocent victims lined the streets, with desperate pleas from loved ones regarding those who now were all gone. Thousands of crosses, candles, and flowers filled the hollow empty streets.

It was heart-wrenching to see the drawings from children to their missing parent. I knew these precious children would never see those parents again.

I was feeling everything. Not only my own unbelievable loss, but others' as well. It was more than I could bear as I watched others facing their pain, grieving like I'd never seen before. I prayed that people could just find a glimpse of Christ to comfort them, to give them strength. I wondered how anyone could get through such a horrific tragedy without knowing that their loved one was in heaven, knowing that they were never going to suffer again as they did on that terrible day. I couldn't fathom a life without hope or without knowing where Steve was spending his eternity.

Steve's family and I began to plan his funeral. It had never occurred to me, with Steve's parents living in different states, that we would need to have multiple memorial services.

The first service was held on September 27 in Basking Ridge, New Jersey, our hometown. Steve's mother wanted it to be at held at the Catholic Church. This was very important to her, and I wanted to respect her wishes. I asked her if she would mind if our pastor could help officiate along with their priest. She wasn't opposed, knowing that Steve and I had been attended a Baptist church for quite some time. I wanted everyone who attended his service to know that Steve was saved by the blood of Christ, and he was in heaven. There was no doubt in my mind where he was, but I needed everyone else to know as well. I wanted them to experience the same peace I had.

I knew that I had to speak at his funeral. I'd never been able to speak in public, but I wanted the gospel proclaimed. I knew God would equip me with what I needed to say.

As the beautiful church filled, bagpipes began to play. These talented musicians had volunteered their time to play before every service in our township. To this day, every time I hear bagpipes, it brings me back to the moment of walking into the service to say goodbye to the man I loved, the man I was going to spend my forever with.

Everyone in that church was still in such disbelief that something so horrific could have happened to someone so young and full of life. Steve's larger-than-life presence was such a huge void, in this room that was filled with so many lives he'd touched. Steve was the guy who would always remember the mailman on Christmas, and all the tellers at our local bank. He was beyond special. He was going to be missed by many.

With complete composure, I stepped up to the podium, as I looked out to see the room filled with many familiar faces. I saw the tears in their eyes and began to speak. I don't even know what I said that day, but I do know that it was not me speaking, but God's Holy Spirit speaking through me. There's no way, after everything I'd gone through, that I would be able to mutter a single word. All I did was make myself available for God to use me. I had a strength that could come only from God.

I know there were actually people angry that I was so composed and put together, rather than sobbing in hopeless despair. It seemed like that's what some people wanted from me. All I wanted was for Steve's death to not be in vain. I wanted people to come to know Christ though this heinous act of violence.

Almost everyone in the room that day had multiple funerals to attend. Everyone was linked to the Twin Towers in some way. Everyone had lost someone, whether husband, wife, father, mother, sister, brother, or friend.

It seemed that everywhere I looked in the weeks that followed, there were funeral processions. And the sound of bagpipes.

Big Mama's whole family had come up to attend the service. They all loved Steve dearly. After the funeral, Big Mama made the decision to return to Texas with her family. It hadn't been the fun week that she signed up for, but she'd been the kind of friend anyone would be blessed to have. She'd seen and experienced pain that would have looked different from her home in Texas. She had been selfless as she took care of my family's needs. She was an angel in the midst of 9/11.

Steve second funeral was in a small quaint church in Monticello, New York, where his father, Jack, lived with his longtime companion, Margaret. Jack had retired from his life on Wall Street years before and moved to Upstate New York to open an Italian restaurant. A heavy deep sadness filled the room. I was incredibly burdened for Jack. This giant man, shaken to the core by his son's death, was so broken. I wondered if he would ever be the same again. Jack, the one person Steve faithfully called every morning before the bell rang on Wall Street, would never again get that call from his son. My heart broke to think about how many mornings Jack would instantly look at the clock, thinking it would be time for Steve to call, then remembering the reality that his phone would not be ringing.

There was also an evening community memorial held in Basking Ridge, New Jersey. This was for the town's nineteen residents who had lost their lives, a time for the community to come together to remember their loved ones who had fallen. Downtown Basking Ridge was blocked off. At the end of the street stood a large white church. On the steps of the church there were individual photos of each victim. They were covered with flowers, letters, and candles that illuminated the sky. I remember having Jacqueline in her stroller as we made our way down to the picture of Steve. As we lit our candle placing it beside the hundreds of others, I knew this was going to be the longest journey of our lives.

At the beginning of October, a memorial service was held in New York's Central Park. This was a private service for the families of the Cantor Fitzgerald employees who lost their lives. Of the many tenants in the towers that had lost so much on that dreadful day, Cantor Fitzgerald had lost the most—658 employees who occupied floors 101–105 of the North Tower were killed. Although thousands of family members attended this memorial, it somehow felt like an intimate gathering. Most of the employees at Cantor Fitzgerald knew one another and, like Steve, had been with the firm for years. These men and women had a tight-knit bond.

Mary Kay attended this service with me. She'd been an unbelievable friend to me in so many ways. Her own husband, Bob, had passed away only months before 9/11. Steve had been there for her and her two precious children, and now she was there for Jacqueline and me. She was at the memorial service not only to support me, but also because she, too, had lost many close friends and acquaintances on 9/11.

Mary Kay's good friend, Melissa, who I'd gotten to know over the past couple of weeks, also attended this service. Melissa's fiancé had worked for Cantor Fitzgerald and had lost his life.

Between the three of us, Mary Kay, Melissa, and I, we shared an instant bond of grieving the men we loved dearly, a bond we would never have chosen.

Looking around us at this service, we could tell people were obviously still experiencing shock and disbelief. I walked around and heard story after story of how families were ripped apart instantly. A woman who worked at Cantor told a story of how she'd planned to go in early the morning of 9/11, but received a call saying her meeting had been canceled. Others overslept, and some were on vacation—stories of how God spared the lives of the few who weren't in the building that day.

Not only did Cantor Fitzgerald take a huge personal loss of family members and employees, but many wondered how the firm was going to survive after such a devastating loss. However, they were not only able to climb out of the pit of 9/11, they also financially assisted the victims' families with the Cantor Fitzgerald Relief Fund. I was truly rooting for Cantor, because Steve had invested more than eighteen years of his life with this firm. I wanted them to succeed. And without Cantor Fitzgerald, I would never have met Steve.

The following week, I traveled back to Dallas for Steve's fifth and final memorial service. The weeks had been physically and mentally exhausting, but Steve had grown close to so many people in Dallas that I felt they needed closure too. This service was held at my home church, where Steve and I had been married and where he'd been baptized.

Earlier that week, the church office had received a strange phone call. The caller asked the secretary if the church was holding a service for a 9/11 victim, and if there would be a body for viewing. This scared us and raised suspicion. At this point, we even considered canceling the service for fear that something might happen, but we decided we didn't want to live in fear. Taking precautions, local authorities were contacted. We had private security for the nearly four hundred people who attended.

The service was officiated by our longtime pastor, Brother Glenn Meredith. Of course, there was deep sadness in the room, but this service was more of a celebration of Steve's life. We celebrated the fact that to be absent from the body is to be present with the Lord (2 Corinthians 5:8). One of my closest family friends sang "I Can Only Imagine," a song about meeting our Savior face-to-face. We were all filled with the knowledge that this separation from Steve was only temporary. We all knew where Steve was.

Each new day was a roller coaster ride of heavy emotions. While I was still in Texas for the final service, late one night a government representative came to give us the news that Steve's body had been found in the midst of the rubble.

All the family members of the victims had provided DNA in hopes of locating the bodies of their loved ones or anything identifiable. For some victims, only a body part was found, unrecognizable. Others were identified by dental records. Many were never found. Of the almost three thousand men and woman who died on 9/11, it's said that remains for 40 percent of them have still not been identified.

Several people, including Honey, had been praying specifically that Steve's body would be found. She knew that it would give me closure.

Since I was in Dallas for Steve's final memorial service, Steve's brother, JJ, had to go and identify his brother's body for the authorities. I don't know how JJ was able to do this, but I'm thankful he did. I know this took a toll on JJ, and that the image of his brother's body wasn't something he would easily be able to forget.

But God had given us closure.

People would often ask me what I thought happened on that day in the World Trade Center. Did I think that my thrill-seeking husband jumped? I'd seen pictures of Steve skydiving before in New Zealand, and it was reported that hundreds of people jumped to their death. There were speculations that Steve was seen in the stairwell.

I will never know. Nor would knowing make me feel any less pain. I do know, without a doubt, that he did all he could to get home to us.

As for Steve's call to me that morning—yes, I do have regrets about not hearing the phone ring. I've beat myself up over it, but it would not have changed the outcome. One thing I'll never regret was my decision to erase the message that Steve left. No one will ever have to hear the fear I heard in Steve's voice that day, especially my precious Jacqueline.

Returning home to New Jersey with Jacqueline and my mother by my side, I felt lost somewhere in the twilight zone. I was walking, talking, and remaining composed, but I wasn't really there. It had been almost six weeks since Steve's death, and I truly didn't know how to go on living without him. Everything was a reminder of my great loss, but what was the hardest thing to me was how the world went on day after day as usual. Didn't the rest of the world know that it was supposed to stop? But the world would keep moving. Bills had to be paid, laundry had to be done, groceries had to be in the house.

I was so thankful for my mother who kept my world afloat. I would try to do simple things like going to the grocery store, but it was difficult for me to focus, and everyday living was exhausting. I really didn't want to cook, and I didn't care a thing about eating.

Friends and neighbors were so gracious as they continued to bring meals for us and take Jacqueline out for playdates. Mary Kay would come over several times a week to make us wonderful gourmet meals and spend time with us. I felt God's hands all around me with the precious people He'd placed in my life.

Even though I knew God was going to take care of us, happiness was not in sight. It was so painful to do anything normal. I felt so alone. It genuinely hurt even to breathe.

I hid my pain well. I remember in the middle of October going to a pumpkin patch with our neighbors. On the outside, I probably seemed like I was doing okay, but it was all I could do to get through the day. I wanted to do things with Jacqueline, so her little life would seem as normal as possible, but I was hurting inside and missed her daddy desperately.

Walking into our big empty house every night, not having Steve there in his favorite chair, was such a huge void. I longed for family dinners and our nightly walks through our neighborhood.

By far the hardest thing to watch was my baby girl running to the back door each night at five o'clock, pressing her tiny face up to the window as she called for her daddy. This was excruciating to watch, night after night.

Weeks had turned into months, and it was incredibly difficult to live in our home without Steve. There were certain rooms in our house I didn't even want to walk into. Every part of the house was consumed with memories and thoughts of Steve. We'd built this home together; now all the plans we had for our lives there were shattered.

Honey never left our side; she'd completely given up her own life in Texas to take care of us. She wouldn't have it any other way.

Steve's family was dealing with their own grief in their own way. I guess being around Jacqueline and me made it harder for them, because we rarely saw them. I thought that after Steve's death, his mother Vera would want to spend more time with Jacqueline, but maybe it was too difficult for her. It was hard for me to understand, but then again, her loss was so great. I couldn't fathom losing a child.

It was becoming increasingly clear that without Steve, maybe New Jersey was not my home. Maybe it was time for us to be back in Texas, something I'd dreamed about for years— though not like this. Not without Steve.

CHAPTER 10

He said to me, "My grace is sufficient for you,
for my power is made perfect in weakness."
Therefore I will boast all the more
gladly of my weaknesses,
so that the power of Christ may rest upon me.

2 CORINTHIANS 12:9 ESV

A s the weeks passed, it was painfully obvious that I couldn't live in our home and raise Jacqueline there without Steve. Our home seemed cold and empty; it had become a place I didn't want to be. I'd met so many wonderful friends who loved us dearly and would do anything for us, but their lives were moving on. I knew I needed to be back in Dallas where I had the support of my family in raising Jacqueline. Our home was not our home anymore. Every hope, every dream, I'd ever had about raising a family with Steve and growing old together had vanished in an instant on September 11. I knew the home we'd built together would never be the same for me.

Steve had always taken such great care of Jacqueline and me that I never had to learn how to do many things on my own.

I began to look through paperwork, financial statements, and bills, trying to make sense out of all that Steve had taken care of daily. I felt completely defeated with all the responsibility that was now mine. Steve had worked hard and saved money all his life. I never realized how much money we spent, and I felt like it was disappearing quickly with our monthly overhead. I wasn't mentally ready to go back to work, and I didn't know if I wanted to go back into New York City ever again. I knew I could never make enough money to support the lifestyle Steve had afforded for us.

Steve's financial adviser assured me that we were going to be okay, but I still had concerns. I began to pray that God would direct me. I knew that living in Texas would cost a third of what we'd been spending living in the Northeast. Strong emotions filled my mind with what-ifs, including guilt about leaving this life behind. I hadn't realized until much too late that I should have embraced New Jersey and my wonderful life there. My lack of contentment had caused me to wish my life away, and now I just wanted to have my life back.

I needed to get away from it all. We decided to fly to Dallas to spend the weekend. Getting away from New York and New Jersey felt good. When I went back to Texas, it was like I could escape reality for a moment. Even though people in other parts of the country had suffered greatly, it was much different than actually being in the midst of the storm.

In Texas, Honey tried to keep me busy and my mind occupied at all times. It seemed like the busier I was, the less time I had to think about all that had happened.

That Sunday after church, we decided to go look at model homes just outside Dallas in an upcoming area called Heath.

Going to look at open houses and model homes had always been one of my favorite pastimes. Just months before, one weekend while Steve and I were visiting Texas, we went to a Parade of Homes, an event where several builders showcase their building styles. They sell tickets to the event to raise money for different charities. People then walk through the houses and vote for their favorite home. There are usually about five to seven homes to tour. I could spend hours walking through each house, getting new ideas. I must say this was not one of Steve's favorite things to do on a Sunday afternoon, he would much rather have been watching a football game somewhere.

But on this day, just months before 9/11, he appeased me for a few hours as we walked through each house, looking for decorating ideas for our new home. Steve always seemed to be shocked by the price of homes in Texas. It was amazing to him how big a house you could get for your money, much different from up north. I remember him jokingly saying to me, "I think I'll buy two of them."

That afternoon, one house in particular caught our attention. We walked through every room and concluded that this was the house we would be voting for as our favorite. We stayed in this house just a little bit longer and snapped pictures, so we could duplicate decorating ideas for our new home in New Jersey. Most of the houses we viewed that day were for sale, but this one had already sold. We could definitely see why.

Months later, here I was in the same neighborhood, this time without Steve. I wasn't looking to buy a home—just trying to stay busy and pass the time. As we drove through the neighborhood looking to see if there were any new homes to explore, we drove past the house Steve and I had voted for as our favorite months before. I noticed a "For Sale" sign in the front yard. I told my mom to stop. My heart began to beat a little faster.

Honey, Jacqueline, and I decided to walk up to the front door. I cannot explain the warm feeling we all experienced as we walked through the door. Once inside, we met the builder. He explained to us that the house had sold months before, but the contract had fallen through. It was back on the market, and he'd discounted it for a quick sale.

I picked up the flyer that was lying on the kitchen counter. On it was a photo of the house, along with the asking price, which had been marked down significantly. I felt like I knew how much I should spend on a new home, but never thought it would be this soon. I had an exact number in my mind, and I didn't want to go a penny over it. This house's original price was over my budgeted amount, but the new discounted price was under it.

Was it just a crazy coincidence that the house was back on the market and within my budget? Or was this God? Steve himself had been in this home, and he thought the original asking price was more than fair. So in my mind, I had his approval.

Honey, Jacqueline, and I decided to walk through the house. It was painted in basically the same colors that I'd spent eight months choosing for our home in New Jersey, and this was the house I'd gotten some of my decorating ideas from. In the media room, the TV was playing my favorite movie of all time, *Top Gun*. It was like this house was built for us with all the details large and small.

As we drove away, I glanced at the street sign. The name of the street was Kings Pass, while the name of my street in New Jersey was Kings Ridge.

I was a little excited; I didn't even know I could feel this emotion, after all I'd gone through. I felt like God was giving me little signs. His fingerprints seemed to be everywhere I turned. I had such a strange peace that this was where Jacqueline and I needed to be. I just wanted to make sure that this was from God, and not some silly thing I'd worked up in my own mind. I didn't want to make any irrational moves without totally being in God's will.

I hadn't sold my house in New Jersey. I hadn't even thought about putting it on the market. I didn't know a thing about buying or selling a house.

We went back to my parents' home, and as I told everyone about the house, they could tell I was enthusiastic about it. But I was scared to make such a big move without a clear leading from the Lord. That night, I prayed, seeking God's will. Asking God to give me wisdom.

The next day, before we headed to the airport, we decided to drive by the house once again. I wanted to see it one more time before I went back to New Jersey. As we drove up to take one last peek, we saw a landscaping company in the front yard putting in seasonal color. They were planting several flats of pansies in the front flower beds. My heart almost stopped, because these seasonal flowers had a special place in my heart.

For as long as I could remember, my mother had been in a prayer group. This group of ladies had all been in Bible study together for many years. They were all the closest of friends and shared an incredible bond because of their love for Christ. One of the ladies in the prayer group, Charlotte, had a son who'd gone through a tough time in his adolescent years, when he struggled with addiction. His godly parents weren't going to allow this rebellion in their home. The boy spent many nights sleeping in his car as a consequence. I cannot imagine how difficult this must have been for his parents. But they knew they had to apply tough love while continuing to pray for him and trusting God to deliver him and take care of him. God's Word promises that if you train up a child in the way he should go, then even when he is old, he will not depart from it (Proverbs 22:6). His family stood firm on God's Word.

Charlotte asked her prayer group to pray for her son every time they saw a pansy. So, every time anyone in this powerful group of prayer warriors would see a pansy, they would pray for Charlotte's son to turn from his rebellion. God answered the prayers of this sweet family, and their son was set free. God was there to protect him through everything he'd gone through.

This story had always been such a beautiful testament to me of God's unfailing love, even through our toughest trials. That morning seeing the pansies being planted reminded me of God's perfect love and protection. I knew that whatever Jacqueline and I had to endure, God would be there to get us through.

Taking a big step of faith, I went inside and signed the papers to buy the house. We headed back to New Jersey and let everyone know we were moving to Texas. I don't think this came as a surprise to anyone. I do think the next thing I told them was a bit of a shock: that we were moving to Texas in just three weeks, because I wanted us to be settled there before Christmas. I didn't know how this was going to happen, but I knew God was in control.

We had a dear friend who was a realtor. It was comforting to know that she was going to be able to help sell our house. I explained to her that we were moving out in three weeks, and that I needed to sell the house before I moved. She completely understood that I didn't want to carry two mortgages, but she said she didn't know if she would be able to sell the house that quickly. We both knew it was a very unique home, much different from most homes in New Jersey at the time. Most people were looking for a traditional or colonial style home. Our home was far from that. She encouraged me not to move out before the house sold, knowing the house would show much better fully furnished.

No one really knew what would happen to the American economy after 9/11, but I knew one thing: I was downsizing. I knew exactly how much Steve had invested in the house. In selling it, I wasn't trying to make money, but just trying to be smart and not lose money.

I told the realtor how much I wanted to put the house on the market for. Everyone thought the price was high, if I wanted it to sell quickly. I stuck with my asking price and with my decision to move out in three weeks. Everyone around me continued to tell me not to get my hopes up—that in three weeks, it would be almost impossible to sell my house, do inspections, close, and move out.

I guess I should've been a little concerned, but I wasn't. I continued to pray. Within three days, we had three offers. When the world said, "You can't sell that house in three weeks," God was saying, *I can sell it in three days!*

CHAPTER 11

J ust three short weeks after putting our home on the market, it was time to move. We were beyond blessed that the Red Cross was going to help with the move back to Texas.

I remember walking around the empty house after everything had been moved out. It brought me back to a precious time with Steve. I remembered how excited we both were the night before we moved into our new home, as we sat on the empty staircase planning our forevers. Now someone else was going to get to make their memories in our home.

It was so hard to say goodbye to Steve's family, our friends, and all the hopes and dreams that we would be leaving behind. I hadn't expected it would be so difficult to leave New Jersey, especially after all those years of my wanting to be back in Texas—but never like this. Everyone promised to keep in touch. They all wanted us to find happiness.

After arriving at our new house in Heath, we had an army of friends and family there to help us get settled in. Big Mama's husband, Mike, worked hard to make sure the new garage was put together just the way Steve would have had it. He knew how meticulous Steve had kept his garage in New Jersey. He went to great lengths to make sure our garage in Texas was organized with the same amount of detail. It looked almost as if Steve had done it himself.

Throughout the house, every box was unloaded within days, and every picture hung in just the right place. Honey wasn't going to sleep until everything was perfect. Everyone wanted us to feel settled quickly, and we did.

I jumped right back into being involved in the church that I'd grown up in. It was such a bittersweet feeling to be home. Our church family had been praying for us daily since 9/11. They knew that God was going to take care of us. They could see His power in our lives, by the strength He was giving us day by day.

My pastor, Brother Glenn, asked if I would be willing to share my testimony at our annual Christmas program, which was going to be called "The Gift of Hope." Everyone around us knew that I'd placed my hope in Jesus Christ and that He was the one getting us through. I didn't even have to think about it. I wanted to share with everyone what God had been doing in my life.

On that December night, I walked up to the front of the church to tell my story. I spoke about how God had been with me since the moment the towers fell, how He'd never left my side, and how He had given me peace and hope in a completely hopeless situation. Looking back, I can't fathom how I was able to do this only three months after my world had been shaken to the core. It was God! Truly, a living God was using me as His vessel.

Christmas was only weeks away. It was no secret to anyone that it had always been my favorite time of the year, but I had no idea how I was going to get through this holiday season without Steve by my side. Thanksgiving was somewhat bypassed because our loss was simply so raw, but with a young child in my home, I couldn't pretend that Christmas wasn't happening. Yet how could we get through Christmas without Steve? I couldn't even grasp the concept of Christmas morning without him being there with Jacqueline and me.

I once again looked to the Lord to get us through, and I focused on my sweet baby girl. My heart was still so pained for her.

To get through the weeks leading up to Christmas, I shopped. I bought Jacqueline everything her little heart desired, which usually consisted of her pointing at the television and saying, "Mom, I want that, Mom, I want that." She was so precious to me. I felt like as long as we kept the environment around her somewhat normal, she was going to be okay. We were surrounded by the unconditional love of family at all times, and if I wasn't having a good day, someone was there to rescue Jacqueline so she wouldn't have to see my pain.

Christmas traditions had always been very important in my family. Every Christmas Eve my family went out to dinner, then returned home to open our Christmas pajamas, and we always had a birthday cake for Jesus. We would sing "Happy Birthday," and end our night by putting out cookies and milk for Santa. The next morning, after a breakfast casserole, we would sit around the Christmas tree opening gifts together. This Christmas would be much different. Everyone knew there wasn't going to be anything normal about it.

Big Mama's husband, Mike, helped us get through this first Christmas. Big Mama and her family had been having a carnival-style Christmas for years. They called it Carnie Christmas. It felt like everyone was grieving differently, and Mike's way of grieving was getting to work. Both my family and Big Mama's family spent the night together at my house on Christmas Eve. We ordered pizza and assembled gifts for Jacqueline.

On Christmas morning, my house had been transformed into a carnival by Mike and my dad. That morning was nothing close to our traditional Christmas. We played games to get gifts. There was a string pull, where you would pull a string and your gift would be whatever was on the other side of the curtain. We dropped water balloons from my second-story balcony to see who could drop them into the hula-hoop below. And you couldn't have a carnival without throwing darts and busting balloons.

It was a Christmas morning of crazy games and goofy outfits, pure carnival style—untraditional Christmas fun. It was such a wonderful distraction from our normal Christmas, which would have been too painful to endure.

We laughed and played with Jacqueline. This was exactly what my family needed, and *when* we needed it. It gave us a chance to be so silly that for the moment we could lose ourselves in the fun. We didn't have a chance to think back on the tragedy that had struck our family just months before. I really believe this was the only way my family could have made it through Christmas 2001.

In the following month, I was starting to become overwhelmed, increasingly aware that I was incapable of running a household. All the important tasks in my life had always been taken care of by Steve or by my mother. I never had to think about a thing. It was probably time for me to learn these things for myself, but I was having a hard time concentrating. Most of the time, even returning phone calls seemed difficult for me. So paying bills, balancing checkbooks, and looking over investment statements was completely blowing my mind. I felt like I was capable only of taking care of Jacqueline and myself.

Once again, my mother stepped up to the plate and helped me get through this season in my life without my electricity being shut off—not because I didn't have the money to pay the bills, but because I simply couldn't remember to pay them.

We chose to stay extremely busy, and my cooking skills that I'd worked so hard on went downhill. We were never home and went out for every meal. Nighttime was the hardest for me. I'd always loved our family time at the dinner table with Steve, when we would sit and talk about our day. So being home in the evening looking at the empty seat at the table wasn't going to be an option.

I knew that we were under God's constant protection, and I continued to feel His presence in so many ways. The outpouring of support from everyone in Texas, New Jersey, and New York was amazing. People I'd gone to school with, modeled with, and gone to church with—all were praying for us and sending their love. The compassion and love from all over the world, from people who didn't even know us, was incredible. My mailbox was flooded with cards, letters, and gifts. It was as if the world was wrapping its arms around us and praying for us.

We felt every prayer. I felt God faithfully shielding us from the real pain of what had happened on that September day.

Precious children from all over the country wrote letters to Jacqueline, drew pictures for her, and sent her teddy bears and stuffed animals. Some sweet lady even made her a blanket. Hours of work and love went into this hand-knitted blanket from someone who had never met us.

Suzy Calhoun, Heath Calhoun's sweet Christian mother, wrote me a heartfelt note expressing her sorrow for the loss of my husband. She said that she too had lost her husband just years before, on September 11, 1995, and she was praying for us.

My dearest friend Lizabeth sent a very personal letter to Jacqueline, one that I'll never forget. Her own daughter had been born just days before Jacqueline. Our families had celebrated the girls' first birthdays together. Lizabeth had gone into great detail in writing Jacqueline, to let her know how very special she was to her daddy. She mentioned some very personal moments that she'd noticed about the two of them together. She wanted Jacqueline to have personal knowledge of her daddy when she was old enough to be able to comprehend why her daddy was no longer with her.

I cherished this letter and others with all my heart. Lizabeth and so many other people had reached out to us, showed me true examples of God's people at work to help one another heal. In reality, it would be years before I could bring myself to open and read all the sweet and kind comforting notes—not from lack of genuine appreciation, but because reading each one meant I had to face our new reality.

Honey kept track of the multitudes of cards and letters. She kept them safe for me, so I could read them one by one when my heart was ready.

Of my many blessings, one of the greatest was my mother. God had given me such a gift when he made her my mother. She'd always been my best friend and the perfect godly mother to guide me through every step of life. Now she had unselfishly given up her own life to continue taking care of Jacqueline and me. She played so many different roles in my life during this time. God knew that I was going to need someone strong and selfless, and that was my mom—my Honey. I would never have made it through such a difficult time without her by my side. I know it may sound like a cliché, but she was honestly the wind beneath my wings.

In the months that followed, doors began to open for me to speak and share my story. I knew this was God's handiwork and not my own. Just weeks before I'd left New Jersey to move back to Texas, I'd been interviewed by a Christian organization called Campus Crusade for Christ. I later learned that my interview had been published and turned into a color brochure. This organization had been passing out the brochure for months near Ground Zero. It had been published in several languages. Now I was being asked to speak at churches and major Christian events all over the United States. I would have the opportunity to share my story about what had happened on that dreadful day and to tell people how I was able to continue on.

I began to travel for speaking engagements. Everyone wanted to hear about how someone could have lived through such a horrific day while still having hope for the future. If I could tell this story and give hope to anyone going through a tragedy, then that's what I wanted to do.

Opportunities for me to speak and to tell my story were being presented to me daily. I didn't have any public speaking experience. My stomach was in knots at the thought of speaking in front of large crowds. But I knew this was what I was supposed to be doing with my life.

Through Campus Crusade for Christ, I flew to South Dakota and spoke to a large audience at a "See You at the Pole" rally. As thousands of college students packed the room, I shared my beautiful love story. I talked about the peace and comfort God had given me since the moment the towers fell. I spoke about God's promises—His promise to be a father to the fatherless and His promise to give me a hope and a future (Jeremiah 29:11). When the invitation was given, hundreds of students walked forward and made personal decisions to accept Jesus Christ as their Lord and Savior. It was nothing I said; it was all about what Christ did on the cross.

Steve hadn't died in vain. God was going to use Steve's life and death for His glory! I realized then that what Satan meant for evil on 9/11, my God was going to use for good!

What I felt that day was an undeniable sense of purpose, an intense high that people long for and a closeness to The Living God which only comes from knowing Jesus Christ. As long as I was telling my story, with Jacqueline and Honey by my side, I could go on.

CHAPTER 12

Do not be afraid or discouraged,

for the LORD will personally go ahead of you.

He will be with you;

he will neither fail you nor abandon you.

DEUTERONOMY 31:8 NLT

lthough Jacqueline and I had a wonderful new home in Texas, it soon just became home base. We were rarely home the first year, due to accepting invitations to speak and share my testimony. Steve's life and our experiences after 9/11 continued to drive me day by day in our busy new lifestyle.

Every time I spoke, I encouraged people to live in the moment, to not take life for granted, and to be content. I'd dealt with this issue of contentment for years before 9/11 and had finally come to terms with it. I finally understood that we're supposed to grow where God plants us. I wanted to do everything I could to make amends for my past, for all that I'd taken for granted. I'd realized much too late that I should have been content with all God had blessed us with. I wanted to do everything possible to make Steve proud and to represent him well.

When I didn't have a speaking engagement, I was busy planning trips for Jacqueline, Honey, and me. We would often pack our bags, hop on a flight, and go wherever our hearts desired. We didn't have a set schedule keeping us from being able to go and do as we pleased. That first year, we visited New Jersey often. It was very important to me to remain close to everyone there.

I know there was a part of me that was afraid of what I would feel if I slowed down long enough to think about it. Honey was always up for anything that would keep me occupied. She knew it was inevitable that at some point, I'd have to settle down and face the overwhelming grief.

Although my sweet Jacqueline was loved and doted on by many, I continued to feel sorry for her. I couldn't imagine living life without a father's love. I felt like she'd had enough taken away from her, and it was my job to give her the world.

With our jet-setting lifestyle, Jacqueline didn't have any real structure or boundaries of any kind in her life. I don't think she knew the word no. She got everything she wanted, when she wanted it. Honey was the worst at spoiling her, always giving Jacqueline anything she wanted. Honey always said, "Now why would she need to share, when we can buy her one." Our world revolved around Jacqueline. She never had any consequences for wrong actions. She wasn't a bad child, but everyone around her was turning her into a very spoiled one.

I knew in my heart that Steve would have wanted her to have structure and discipline. Giving Jacqueline the world wasn't going to bring her daddy back. This is something I would struggle with for years, overcompensating for our daughter's incredible loss. I wanted so badly to give her the tools she would need to cope with in this world without a father, but I wasn't sure I knew how.

At times, life was increasingly frustrating. I began experiencing anger over the fact that Steve had been taken away from us. Night after night, I dreamed about him, always the same dream. In my dream, Cantor Fitzgerald had invited all the 9/11 victims' families to Disney World. Jacqueline and I and all the other families were standing in a large area in front of Cinderella's castle. Several men approached the large stage and said they had a big surprise for everyone. They asked the crowd to count down. As we all counted down—five, four, three, two, one—suddenly all the men and women who'd lost their lives on September 11 walked out from behind the stage. Everyone cheered as hundreds of men and woman entered the crowd to be reunited with their loved ones.

As Steve approached Jacqueline and me, smiling with his gigantic grin, he said, "It was just a big joke! It was all just a big trick. We fooled everyone." I was so confused and upset with him. I thought it was the worst prank anyone could possibly do. I told Steve how devastated we'd all been and about all the nights I'd cried myself to sleep. I asked him, "How could anyone do this to people they love?"

Night after night, I continued having this dream. It was such an unsettling dream and seemed so real.

Of course, I was angry that such a horrific act of violence had taken Steve from us. Being a believer in Christ didn't mean I didn't go through all the emotions of grief. My family had been ripped apart. There were days when I was crushed, defeated, depressed, and angry. But every morning when I pulled myself out of bed, I realized I had something not everyone had. Being a believer meant that I had hope; I wasn't just looking at my future and wishing my life would somehow turn out okay. I was looking at my Lord and Savior, knowing that His Word said that my future would be truly good. Day after day, I had to die to what I felt, and I had to live by what God's Word said. I continued to depend on God and His promises.

I started regularly attending a grief group at a church nearby. I realize that people everywhere had gone through such suffering and loss. I thought that by moving back to Texas, I could somehow escape the feeling of being surrounded by grief, but I could not. Many of the people who attended the group were not Christian. To me, their pain seemed unbearable. They lived hopeless lives, unable to deal with the heavy grief they carried each day. My heart began to hurt for these people who'd spent a lifetime being unable to move forward. I realized how blessed I was to serve a God who carried my burdens for me, a God who never left my side, a God who "heals the brokenhearted and binds up their wounds" (Psalm 147:3 NIV).

When it had been almost a year since 9/11, I was ready to go back to work. Modeling and public speaking were the only jobs I'd really ever had. Nancy Campbell, my agent in Dallas, had kept up with us all these years and was painfully aware of all we'd gone through. She was ready to put me back to work. I started working immediately, for some old clients and some new ones. I worked while Honey took care Jacqueline. It was good for me to experience others treating me as just a person again and not as a victim.

One day I was booked to work for Dillard's just outside Fort Worth. Shooting their newspaper ads had become almost a weekly job for me. One day, after my job was over, I was changing in the dressing room, and I could hear the next group of models coming in. I was used to running into models I'd worked with in the past, friends I hadn't seen in years. It was always great to see them and to catch up.

I was packing my bag, getting ready to leave, and saying goodbye to everyone in my dressing room, when I heard a familiar voice from the other side of the dressing room curtain. "Shelly, is that you?" It was Heath Calhoun.

It had been almost eight years since I'd seen or heard from Heath. I must say that he was still just as gorgeous as the first time I saw him that day at Houston's Restaurant when I was just nineteen. As I began talking with him, it was clear that his authentic demeanor hadn't changed at all. He said he'd found out from Nancy Campbell about the incredible loss of my husband, and he hoped that Jacqueline and I were doing okay. Briefly, he told me that he'd just moved back to Dallas. For the past two and a half years he'd lived in Tyler, Texas, where he'd opened his own health club. He'd recently sold it, because his heart wasn't in it anymore.

He was so real and still had such a playful personality. It was great to see Heath after all these years. He'd always been so easy to talk to, and nothing had changed. We could have talked for hours, but he was on Dillard's clock and was about to start shooting. It seemed like those few minutes weren't enough time to catch up on all the years that had passed. He asked if I'd like to have coffee sometime. This seemed innocent enough, and we exchanged numbers.

Within a few days, Heath called. It didn't take him long to realize I wasn't a morning person. He asked if we could catch up over dinner instead. A couple of days later, we met for dinner.

That night at dinner, we were just two friends having a good time. There was never any awkward feeling of not knowing what to talk about. We were having fun together, laughing, talking about old times. Heath made me feel alive again.

Heath and I had both grown up so much over the past eight years. I was now able to handle his playful personality. And that night at dinner, I saw a side of him I'd never known. The fun, flirty guy I once knew had a much more serious side to him. And Heath—who'd known the very naive, fun-loving Shelly—was now seeing a much more in-depth side of me that hardly anyone had known. Heath wanted to know more.

As the weeks went on, we continued to hang out with one another. I poured out my heart to him about Steve and all that I'd gone through. Heath was such an incredible listener. Somehow he was able to make me talk about things I'd kept bottled up. It was like having my own private therapist. He was so incredibly easy to talk to, and he made me feel like I could tell him anything. At home, in my family room, Heath, Honey, and I would stay up all night long talking.

Though Heath and I were just friends, I started to have intense guilt about spending time with him. I wouldn't hang out with him in public for fear that someone might see us together and think we were dating. We both knew our friendship could easily turn a corner. There was definitely something there besides a strong friendship.

Heath decided to plan a spontaneous weekend trip for the two of us to Santa Fe. The night before the trip, I knew in my heart of hearts that I couldn't go. My heart belonged to Steve. I called Heath and told him I couldn't go with him to Santa Fe. Even though I loved spending time with him and I knew we had something special between us, it was too early to be dating. And I couldn't deal with the guilt I was feeling. I felt like I might be disrespecting Steve somehow just by spending time with Heath.

The next day I drove to Heath's house to tell him I wasn't emotionally ready to start dating. It was incredible how completely understanding of my feelings he was. He knew I still needed time to heal, but he also knew we had something special. He backed away and said that if it was meant to be, God would bring us back together. Heath had been an unbelievable friend to me over the past couple of weeks. He was able to help me with my healing process in a way no one else had been able to. I was going to miss hanging out with him. But I knew I was making the right choice.

As the first anniversary of 9/11 approached, it was hard to believe that a year had already passed. All the family members of the victims were invited to attend a private ceremony to honor their loved ones. The names of nearly three thousand men and women were to be read out loud during the ceremony, which would be televised around the world.

This was a very difficult day. I couldn't bring myself to attend the ceremony in New York City. Even the weeks leading up to the anniversary were hard to bear. It seemed that everywhere I turned, I was having to watch the towers fall to the ground over and over again. Gruesome details I'd never seen were shown repeatedly on television stations. Graphic photos headlined all the newspapers and magazines for weeks. I had to turn away. I couldn't handle watching or seeing the torture the victims had endured. I wished I could somehow be able to fast-forward through this difficult time. I just wanted the day to be over. I was having to relive my worst nightmare day after day.

Waking up on September 12 was a relief; we'd made it through the first anniversary of 9/11. God had been my constant pillar of strength.

That fall, I decided it was time to stop running from reality, and to try and settle down. I put Jacqueline in a Mother's Day Out program twice a week. She needed to be around other children and to have structure. I knew she would be starting kindergarten one day, and she and I both were going to be in shock with a normal daily routine, after we'd been living life on our own time, staying up all hours of the night and sleeping most of the day away. Most nights we stayed up playing games, playing dress up, and watching movies, going to bed around 2:00 a.m. and sleeping in way past lunch time. A little structure was going to be good for both of us.

I spent the next year working on myself. I was honestly trying to find out who I was, now that I wasn't Steve's wife. I'd never been a single woman in the world, and now I was not only a single woman but a single mother.

I hadn't completely stopped public speaking, but I wasn't pursuing it. I was ready for everyone to start looking at me like I was Shelly again, and not a 9/11 widow. I wanted desperately to try to move on with my life. But was I turning away from my true purpose?

I'd remained extremely close to Mary Kay and Melissa. They missed having us close up north, but they were always more than willing to come to Dallas to visit. Wherever we went and whatever we did, we always had fun together.

One weekend when they were in town, I was looking forward to taking them to a true Texas honky-tonk. We were headed to a place called Southern Junction, but we got really lost on our way.

With no navigation, we were driving around on a wild -goose chase. We ended up on a dirt road somewhere outside Dallas and figured we would make the best of it. I pulled over to one of the smallest honky-tonks I'd ever seen, in a small Texas town I'd never even heard of. We were definitely overdressed but walked in and made ourselves at home. Lucky for us, it was Karaoke night. To a crowd full of true cowboys, we belted out "I Will Survive." We had survived. All of us had gone through such suffering and loss, but just being together lightened the load.

I tried to casually start dating. It seemed like everyone was trying to set me up with someone. They just wanted me to be happy. Honestly, I still wasn't emotionally stable enough to date anyone. I would go on a date with a really nice guy, then never return his call. I just wasn't ready. I was still living day by day in a bit of a fog. I think staying up all night and sleeping most of the day away was taking a toll on me. There was just never enough time in the day to get everything done. I was continuing to lose weight and handfuls of hair. I often felt like I was drowning with responsibility, just trying to keep my head above water. Even the simplest task of a normal daily routine overwhelmed me. Honestly, I don't even remember checking my phone messages or paying my bills most of the time. I just didn't want to deal with the responsibility that had been thrust upon me. I somehow hoped it would all go away or someone would just do it for me.

One of my closest friends and I were supposed to meet in LA for a girlfriends' weekend. The whole trip was planned—flights and hotels booked. But I didn't show up. I'd totally forgotten about the trip. Who forgets about trips? I felt horrible. My friend left several messages, but I'd just never checked them until it was too late.

My family was starting to be concerned about my forgetfulness, my lack of concentration, my unhealthy weight, and my inability to complete projects. Honey suggested I go see a doctor. The doctor was sympathetic toward all I'd gone through, and I was put on a low dose of an antidepressant. This was my low!

It was very difficult for me to be put on medication. I'd experienced such amazing strength immediately after 9/11. I'd depended on God daily, and He'd carried me through. Where had I gone wrong? Had I taken my eyes off Jesus? Why was I needing to depend on anything else but the Lord? I knew I needed help, or I'd lose all my friends and never have another date in Dallas again. The medicine definitely helped, and I wasn't feeling so defeated by life—but was I just masking life and reality?

One afternoon, when Mary Kay and Melissa were back in town, we were doing a little retail therapy, hitting all our favorite shops around Dallas. That day I had an audition at the Hotel ZaZa, a cool, swanky hotel. The girls didn't mind tagging along with me. After the audition, as we were walking out of the hotel, I noticed Heath's black truck. We must have somehow missed each other in the audition. I hadn't seen Heath in almost a year, but just seeing his car made my heart beat faster.

The girls saw my giddiness and knew instantly there was something there. They convinced me to leave a note on his car, something I would have been scared to death to do without a little persuasion. The note said, "I would love to see you." Like a silly school girl, I ran and put the note under the windshield wiper of his car. As we drove away, we were giggling like a bunch of teenagers. I wondered how I could have done something so brazen.

Minutes later my phone rang. We were all screaming with excitement, hoping it was Heath. I tried to stay cool as I answered the phone. It was Heath, and we spoke as if no time had passed. I asked him to come meet us for dinner, and he was more than willing.

I knew Mary Kay and Melissa would love Heath. I couldn't wait for them to meet him. They immediately liked him and fell in love with Heath's bold and outgoing personality. They thought it was a great fit for me at this time in my life.

Sparks flew with Heath, and for the third time, we began seeing each other. This time was different. I was more open and actually willing to date. Of course, I was used to spending all my time with Jacqueline and Honey. If Heath wanted to hang out with me, he would have to get used to them being around. Heath was unbelievable with children and they adored him. Jacqueline was no different, and she loved it when Heath came over. He would get on her level and play with her for hours. It was easy to see that Heath was going to be a great dad one day.

One of the things I adored most about Heath was that he was so secure with himself. He'd always known that a piece of my heart would always belong to Steve. He wasn't afraid to talk about that with me. He continued to encourage me to get things out.

Heath and his brother, Blake, had both been adopted. He never once questioned how much he was loved. He'd grown up attending a small Baptist church, very similar to how I was brought up. We both knew all the old gospel songs, and Heath even remembered some of the hymnal page numbers for them. He had a strong, outgoing, straight-shooting personality, and he could talk for hours. He was real, and he didn't take life so seriously. Heath loved to be outdoors riding his Harley or snow skiing. He had an entrepreneur spirit and had moved all over the county. He'd played college football at the University of Central Arkansas, worked on his masters at Colorado State University, got accepted to be an FBI physical fitness instructor in Virginia, attended film school in New York, then lived in LA to pursue acting—and somehow ended up in Dallas. I was glad he had.

We spent a couple of months dating, really getting to know each other. I was crazy about him, and we always had a blast together, but the more time we spent together, the more I realized how different he was from Steve. Sure they were both handsome and loved to be outdoors, but in other ways they were complete opposites. At first it was little things I noticed, like not pulling out my chair for me at dinner, or not coming around to open the car door for me when we were on a date—most of the time just to mess with me. I was used to being treated like a queen, not a buddy. Steve would barely let me carry in groceries. Heath wanted me to pick up the other end of a couch and help him move it. I started to question if this could really ever work out.

My priority in dating was not just looking for someone to date short term. I had Jacqueline, and I couldn't just date someone because they were fun to be with or because we had great chemistry. I had to make sure that whoever I dated was everything I would need in a future husband.

Heath was spontaneous, which was exciting. I loved it at first, but after months of dating, I was having a hard time with it. I craved a schedule, I wanted to have date night reservations and for him to make them. Heath lived by the seat of his pants and never planned anything. He said you miss out on the best things in life if everything's planned.

There were so many things I adored about Heath. He honestly brought me back to the roots of who I really was—but was that who I really wanted to be?

Heath was so different from Steve, and that scared me. He didn't always say what was politically correct but what was on his mind. He was brutally honest, and sometimes I didn't want to hear the truth. He didn't care about what people thought about him. I'd always worried about what everyone thought about everything.

I was old-fashioned, and I loved the thought of the man being in charge. But Heath wanted me to learn how to do things for myself, to be independent. I wanted someone to take care of me the way Steve had and the way Honey did. I didn't want to grow or to learn new things. I didn't care a thing about being independent! That was how I'd always felt loved—when people took care of me. It was truly my love language.

I had so much fun with Heath and adored him, but I knew I couldn't end up with someone so different from Steve.

It seemed like every time I would get close to Heath, something would scare me away. I finally told Heath that I couldn't see him anymore, and that I needed to date other people. Once again, I pushed him away—wondering often why such a great guy with so much going for him would put up with a girl like me.

Thinking I had it all figured out, and knowing what I thought I wanted out of life, I went out looking for it. Somewhere along the way, my life had become more about me and less about God. I shopped day and night, spending way too much money on designer shoes, purses, and anything else I wanted. I started traveling again, but this time with my girlfriends. I went to New York and Los Angeles, got into high profile private clubs, was invited to all the coolest parties, and mingled with the rich and famous. My plate was always overflowing with unbelievable places to go and people to meet, but I still felt a huge void in my life. The more I filled my life with things and not with God, the more empty I felt inside. On the outside, my life looked like something most people would love to have, but deep in my heart there was something missing. I knew I needed to take my eyes off the world and keep them fixed on my Savior. He was the only thing that would fill the void in my heart.

I desperately longed to have love back in my life, but I didn't think it was possible to ever truly love again. I continued to go out on dates and even joined a dating service. I think this was my most desperate attempt to find the love Steve and I had shared. I went on a couple of dates and decided that if these were the only options I had, it was best to remain single for the rest of my life. I dated very successful men who made dinner reservations at all the coolest places in Dallas, lavished me with gifts, and treated me like a queen—guys who fit the mold perfectly of what I thought I was looking for. But I treated them horribly, going days and sometimes weeks without calling them. I compared everyone I dated to Steve, and there wasn't a man on earth who could live up to that.

Surprisingly, my mind would often go back to Heath— but I pushed the thought away, knowing he couldn't possibly be the one.

Honestly, I needed a project, something to keep me busy. Jacqueline was going to start kindergarten soon. I knew this was going to be tough for me. She was my little runaround buddy, and I hated being away from her. I wanted Jacqueline to grow up the same way I had; I graduated high school with the same kids I'd started kindergarten with, and to this day we're still close friends. Jacqueline and I had traveled so much in the past few years, I wasn't even sure she knew where home was. Maybe we needed a fresh start.

One morning I had a modeling shoot on location in a small Texas town called Fairview, just outside McKinney. When I was growing up in Garland, going to McKinney was like driving to Oklahoma, because it seemed so far away. I'd purchased one of my first cars in McKinney. I remember my mother saying, "We're going to drive to the country so we can get a better deal." McKinney wasn't country anymore. It was now one of the fastest growing cities , but Fairview, just a few miles away, was still a little country town. Their town motto was, "Keeping It Country."

I drove up to a beautiful home surrounded by mature trees. It reminded me so much of New Jersey. I kept asking everyone on the set that day, "Where are we? Fairview?" I fell instantly in love with this precious little town. I met the owners of the house where we were shooting, who were down-to-earth and kind. They even had a daughter who was Jacqueline's age and she too would start kindergarten the following year. They spoke highly of the elementary school, which was in the Lovejoy school district. I knew this small-town feel would be a perfect fit for Jacqueline and me.

After leaving the set, I immediately called my good friend Chris. He'd been my next door neighbor growing up, one of my closest childhood friends, and he was now a realtor in Dallas. I told Chris I wanted to move to Fairview and asked him to help me find a house in that area. The stock market had been doing well for years, and I knew that I would be able to spend a bit more on this new house.

Chris wasted no time. We went out looking the next day. We looked at several houses in Fairview, and at the end of the day, we walked through an older home, originally owned by a former Dallas Cowboys player but with other owners since. The interior décor was completely dated: blue-and-white checkered tiles, peach wallpaper, and mirrors everywhere. But I saw such potential in this house that needed so much work. I knew I could make this house unbelievable. For me, it was definitely a fixer-upper—and just the project I needed to keep me busy.

My house in Heath sold quickly, and I was ready to move on, excited about my new project and a new life in Fairview. I completely renovated the Fairview home while Jacqueline and I lived with my parents for almost six months. It was quite the project. I loved spending my time once again picking out paint colors, selecting tile, and buying furniture to fill our home. During my time in Heath, I'd barely known my neighbors. This was going to be different. This was going to be the home Jacqueline and I would finally plant roots in.

After finishing the renovations, the house was absolutely beautiful. I was so proud of it. I was ready to have people over and entertain. This new home was exactly what we needed.

Melissa had fallen in love and was planning a trip to Dallas with her new boyfriend. She'd become such a dear friend over the past years. We'd gone through so much together. I loved hearing the happiness in her voice as she told me all about how fate had brought this wonderful man into her life after a Yankees game in New York. I was overjoyed for her. We planned to meet for dinner at a restaurant near Dallas. I was excited to spend time with Melissa, but I didn't want to be a third wheel. I'd been casually dating another man who I could have invited to dinner, but my thoughts immediately went back to Heath, though I hadn't seen or talked to him in almost two years. I decided to call him out of the blue. We talked like we'd never missed a beat. I told him about Melissa, and asked if he would join us for dinner. He agreed.

Since we had dated last, he'd opened a successful high-end western boutique in Dallas called Cowboy Cool. Everyone from socialites to rock stars and bikers knew about Cowboy Cool. Heath had always been successful at anything he tried, and this was no different.

I'd always been so comfortable around Heath, and I knew this night would be no different. I could just be myself, and I knew the four of us would have a great time.

Melissa arrived in town. I was so excited to see her and to meet her new boyfriend who I'd heard so much about. That night at dinner, watching them together made me realize that she'd found true love. The terrorist attacks on the World Trade Center had not defeated Melissa.

It made me ask myself why I felt such guilt about forming a new relationship, always guarding my heart and never allowing myself to fall in love. I knew that I'd always been crazy about Heath; he'd never been far from my mind. Why was I so afraid? I was afraid of change, afraid of falling in love, but mostly afraid of what everyone else would think. What if they thought I didn't love Steve because I could love someone else?

So many thoughts rushed through my head. Why did Heath even agree to come with me that night? I hadn't spoken to him in two years and had given him the runaround for almost four years. He was so different from Steve; how could it ever really work out?

I finally gave in to the feelings I'd had all along. At dinner, I put my hand on his leg underneath the table, and he reached over, grabbed my hand, and held it for the rest of the night. That night, for the first time, I completely allowed myself to fall into giddiness. He was my person, and I was crazy about him. We ended the night with a kiss and talked for hours.

The next day I was in awesome spirits after spending a wonderful evening with Heath. I had such a great feeling about him. I'd finally let down my guard and was excited to see where this was going to go this time.

I was modeling that day, on set with a couple of other models, and the camera crew was prepping the lights for us to start shooting. A sweet model who had worked in the industry for years was talking about a guy that she was dating. All the models eagerly listened to her as she talked about her upcoming trip to New York with him. I think someone must have asked his name. What came out of her mouth next almost put me into cardiac arrest. She said, "Heath Calhoun."

My heart dropped and was beating enough to burst out of my chest. I don't know how I even finished the shoot that day. I had to get off that set immediately and call him! Not that I thought he'd been sitting around waiting for me for the past two years, but I guess in the back of my mind, I thought he would always be there for me. Not to mention that he'd just kissed me the night before! Kissing to me was something sacred.

When I got to my car, I called him before I even left the parking lot. I told him I needed to talk to him. I asked him to meet me at an outdoor patio restaurant in Dallas. As I drove to meet him, I wondered if it was too late for Heath and me.

We sat outside on the patio, and I poured out my heart to Heath, but this time not about Steve. I told him I was ready—

finally ready—to be fully in a relationship with him. I told him I'd realized this just the night before, at dinner. I was ready to give him 100 percent.

Heath was skeptical. He'd been burned by me several times. He didn't know whether to believe me. Now I was asking him to drop everything to be with me, after two years of not seeing him. He'd always been there for me, but he was so cautious about getting hurt again. The thought of letting me back into his life at this point was a bit scary to him. Heath had always had strong feeling for me, but he didn't want to play games anymore.

Heath told me that the girl he was going to New York with was a very sweet girl, and he couldn't just cancel the trip at the last minute because I finally decided I was ready for a relationship.

We parted ways, and I was devastated. I couldn't stand the thought of not having Heath in my life. He'd been such a rock for me these past four years. But I'd lost my chance of ever finding true love again. I'd known for years that Heath was "my person," but I just hadn't known if that's what I wanted. When I finally decided to let myself love again—it was too late.

I went home in tears and prayed. The thoughts of Heath being in New York with a beautiful model killed me.

I learned later that Heath had immediately started praying about the situation and what to do—praying that God would open his eyes and that God's will would be done. He prayed that, if I was the right girl for him, he would know it and, if I wasn't, that I would go away and stop playing with his heart. He didn't want to go through what he'd gone through with me in the past.

Weeks went by. I decided to go to the MTV Music Awards in Miami with a guy I'd casually been dating. Making sure he understood that I needed my own room, I allowed myself to have a good time in Miami, as I tried to get Heath out of my mind once and for all.

When I returned home from Miami, I was surprised to find that Heath had called and spoken with my mother. He didn't say what he wanted, but Mom said he wanted me to call him.

I called him. He told me that he'd realized the girl he'd gone to New York with was not the girl for him. He told me he'd been praying and that he knew we were supposed to be together. He said he'd always known there was something special about me from the first moment he saw me in Houston's, when I was just nineteen years old.

CHAPTER 13

I will restore to you the years

that the swarming locust has eaten.

JOEL 2:25 ESV

eath and I began dating for the fourth and final time. I thanked God for opening my eyes to what was right in front of me all along. I guess it was just never the right timing before. My heart had not been ready to be in another relationship until now.

Dating Heath after being married to Steve was a much different relationship. These two men were complete opposites. Steve had been more like my mother and would do everything for me. He filled up my car with gas, paid the bills, balanced my checkbook, booked our vacations, made our dinner reservations . . . the list was endless.

I guess it was time for me to grow. I'd grown in my relationship with Christ, learning to trust Him in all situations, but now it was time for me to grow as a person. As I learned to do things on my own, it was empowering. I was learning quickly how to be the independent woman I never thought I wanted to be. And a part of me was actually liking it.

Heath was the product of being adopted and raised by Christian parents in Arkansas. He had fond memories of his dad, Big Dave, driving the same old white pickup truck, without air conditioning, until the tires almost fell off. Big Dave would wake up his sons early on the weekends to begin delivering hospital beds for their family-owned business, Calhoun Medical Supply. Being a Navy veteran, he wanted to make sure he instilled a strong work ethic in his sons.

Big Dave was a physical therapist and had met his wife, Suzy, at the hospital where he helped children with cerebral palsy.

An aneurysm took Big Dave's life on September 11, 1995. It seemed incredible that a calendar date that held such significance in my life was also such a significant day for Heath.

Heath's mother, Suzy, was a kindhearted and strong Christian woman, and she always made sure to have her boys in church hearing God's Word. Heath's parents taught their boys to appreciate everything they were given and to be responsible.

I knew that one day, when I remarried, I wanted someone who would be capable of loving Jacqueline as if she were his own blood. I knew that Heath, being adopted himself, would be able to do this. He would be able to show the same unconditional love he was given when he was adopted.

Dating Heath couldn't have been more fun. We fell completely in love and were like silly kids. He slowed me down. I guess you could say he made me stop and smell the roses. Once again, I wasn't afraid of the simple things in life, like being home for family dinners, taking long walks around the neighborhood, or simply playing in the water hose with Jacqueline. I now realized that all the wining, dining, and world traveling I'd experienced the past couple of years was not what I needed to make me happy.

Heath continued to encourage me to be independent. He also knew that I'd been on medication for the past couple of years, and he encouraged me to get off it. He told me I didn't need to mask my feelings behind medication, but to face my fears head-on.

I went off my medication cold turkey. Do not do this—big mistake! I went through severe withdrawal for almost a week, and during this time I wasn't someone that anyone wanted to be around. But after that tough week, I was glad to be off my medication once and for all, and I realized I didn't need it.

Heath and I had waited long enough for our happiness to begin, and we started talking about marriage only two months after we again started dating. Heath had already been working on a way to ask me to marry him, which would include a short film he was making. His plan was to rent out a movie theater, play the film, and ask me to marry him.

We'd looked at rings, but I had no idea when he was going to ask me.

One night after work, I met him for dinner at a restaurant across the street from his retail store, Cowboy Cool. We started talking about getting married. He said he already had my engagement ring. Heath had always been quite the jokester, so of course, I didn't believe him. I said, "You don't have the ring." He said, "Yes I do, it's in my car." I thought, *There's no way he would leave an engagement ring sitting in his car in a parking lot.*

After dinner, we walked to his car, and I said, "So where's the ring?" He said, "It's under the passenger seat." I walked around to the other side of the car, thinking he was definitely playing a trick on me. To my surprise, when I reached under the seat, I felt a ring box and pulled it out.

My heart began beating so fast, I could almost hear it. This tiny box held my future. I slowly opened it up. It was empty! Typical Heath, playing tricks on me.

He laughed as he told me to check under the driver seat. I played his game and walked around to the other side of the car, reached under the seat, and pulled out a second box. Same story: it was empty.

Heath told me to check the glove box. I was reluctant to try again, but as I was looking in the glove box, he pulled out of his pocket a beautiful cushion-cut diamond ring and asked me to marry him. Of course, I said yes.

As he placed the ring on my finger, there was no sorrow for all that I'd been through, but only hope for a beautiful future. I didn't have to stop loving Steve to be in love with Heath; God had given me a heart that was able to love again. Not just part of a heart, but my whole heart.

Heath was just the man I needed. He was able to understand that I would always love Steve. He was a strong enough man, secure in himself and our relationship, that he was okay with that.

It was important to Heath to get Jacqueline's approval. A few days later, Heath took Jacqueline and me out to dinner. He wanted Jacqueline to feel special, so in a similar way he hid a box in his car for her to find. After she found her box, she opened it up. She too would have her own very special ring from Heath. He asked her if it would be all right if he married her mother. With excitement on her face, she hugged his neck extra tight and said yes.

We were going to be given a second chance at happiness.

Heath didn't want a big wedding. He wanted to go off to a tropical island and make it more of a private affair. I felt differently about this. There were so many people with whom I wanted to be able to celebrate this special time. I talked Heath into having a small wedding in Dallas. We set the date. We were going to be married at the Mansion on Turtle Creek.

It was much more simple and intimate then my first wedding, but equally beautiful. The colors were a mix of ivory and beautiful fall tones—a compromise of everything Heath and I both loved. Heath was busy planning the honeymoon, while I took care of the rest of the details. I couldn't have been happier.

The night of the rehearsal dinner, I started facing an internal battle. It had been a little less than five years since Steve's death. Was it too early for me to be getting remarried? What would everyone say? Would they think I hadn't mourned long enough the loss of my husband? That I was moving on too fast? That I didn't really ever love Steve if I could love again this soon?

I spent most of the rehearsal dinner in the bathroom, crying and wondering if I was doing the right thing. The issue wasn't Heath; I loved him, and I knew I wanted to spend the rest of my life with him. The problem was me, and I believe it was Satan trying to strip me once again of my happiness. I fought back every lie that Satan tried to put in my head. I came to grips with the internal torture that I'd faced for years. I made the decision that I was going to allow myself to be happy again. I knew that Steve would have wanted that, not only for me but also for Jacqueline.

The big day came. I went on with my day as usual. I dropped Jacqueline off at school, went to get my nails done, went back to her school to watch her sing at her kindergarten performance, and then we headed to the Mansion on Turtle Creek to get married. Jacqueline was an important part of the big day. She walked down the center aisle in her precious flowing ivory dress and ballerina flats, and made her way to the front of the room, where she took her seat on the front row next to Honey.

Now it was my turn. As my dad walked me down the aisle, I fixed my eyes on Heath. I could feel all the love in the room. Everyone there had taken care of Jacqueline and me, and had loved us unconditionally. Most importantly, they had prayed for us daily. God had faithfully blessed the broken path that led me to Heath. His sovereign hands had guided me, never leaving my side.

Heath and I exchanged our vows and then rings. I had the inscription "Twice Blessed" engraved inside Heath's wedding band. I truly felt like God had given me a second chance at life and love.

Jacqueline stood and walked toward Heath and me. Heath dropped to one knee to make his own vows to her. He reached in his pocket and pulled out a tiny necklace with a small heart and placed it around her neck. He looked at her as if no one else was in the room and told her he felt like God had put him in our lives for a reason. He said he was going to be there for us. He was going to be the best dad to her he could possibly be.

I'm pretty sure there wasn't a single person in the room that night who didn't shed a tear. It was a precious moment. I'd never seen Jacqueline's sweet little face look so vulnerable as she looked at him with her big brown eyes, taking in every word he was saying.

Our pastor, Brother Glenn, prayed for us as a family and then pronounced Heath and I husband and wife. As the small crowd cheered, I was overcome by God's faithfulness. Knowing this was the hope and future He had promised in His word.

My life was twice blessed—though not entirely the fairy tale I once dreamed about. I had to endure tough trials to get to where I am today, but somehow my shattered dreams lead me to a closer walk with my one true love, Jesus.

How did I get through? By choosing God every day! By praying even when I didn't know what to pray for, and most of all by clinging to the Word of God and by believing it. Even in my darkest days, when I couldn't fathom a future, my God was there to hold me, comfort me, and give me hope.

I'm thankful that what Al-Qaeda and the terrorists meant for evil on 9/11, God in His sovereignty has used for His glory. I've personally seen people come to know Jesus Christ as their Savior through this horrible tragedy.

Looking further back, in my heart of hearts, I know that the only reason I was given the opportunities that came my way in the modeling industry was so that I could meet Steven Gregory Genovese. It was no accident.

And on that final September day when Steve left for work, God knew that Steve wouldn't be coming home to Jacqueline and me. We aren't promised tomorrow. Steve was young and strong, and he had the whole world at his fingertips. I thank God every day that Steve had a personal relationship with Jesus, so that I can take comfort in knowing that he was lifted from the 104th floor straight into the arms of his loving God—the same God who has held me and carried me since the moment the towers fell.

CHAPTER 14

The LORD is good to those whose hope is in him,

the one who seeks him.

LAMENTATIONS 3:25 NIV

The tenth anniversary of 9/11 was right around the corner; it was hard to believe ten years had already passed. Jacqueline was eleven and turning into a beautiful young lady. She had so much going for her. She was my angel. She had long brown hair and was tall and thin, with her daddy's long legs and his unbelievable mind for numbers. She'd recently started getting into theater and playing the piano, and she had a beautiful voice. Steve would have been so proud of her. The world was going to have endless opportunities for this child.

Jacqueline now had a baby brother: David Cash Calhoun, who was about to turn four. Everyone called him Cash. He had shaggy blond hair, and he looked a bit like a little surfer boy. He was sweet, kindhearted, and had a great little personality.

Both these children had been such unbelievable blessings to me. I felt like the broken pieces of my world had been put back together. I never thought that after 9/11 I could ever feel this complete again, but somehow by the grace of God, I did.

We stayed busy with the school schedule and the kids' activities and were able to make it up to New Jersey about once a year. I was now a stay-at-home mom. I enjoyed the wonderful time with my children and the flexibility this gave me. I'd met so many wonderful new friends in Fairview, and I was involved at the schools, in our church, and in a Bible study group.

Meanwhile, 9/11 was something that was always going to be a part of who I was, and it was never far from my mind. I'd tried for many years to just have a normal life and not bring up the painful memories of it, but this year, with the tenth anniversary, it was going to be increasingly difficult to ignore due to all the media hype. Every channel I turned to was promoting documentaries about 9/11. Every magazine in the grocery store checkout line stared at me with pictures of the Twin Towers blazing with fire. As I read some of the stories, I realized how sheltered I really had been. There were so many people who were still stuck in such bad places in their lives; their pain was overpowering.

We'd started attending a church that was closer to our home, Cottonwood Creek Church in Allen, Texas. The pastor's wife, Jeana, was a good friend of one of my girlfriends, Robin. One day we were all at Robin's house, and Jeana asked if I would be willing to speak at Cottonwood Creek on Sunday, September 11, 2011. The church was going to have a tenth anniversary service.

In my mind I thought, *No way!* I hadn't had any speaking engagements since before I married Heath, and I'd honestly planned on never doing it again. It was out of my comfort zone to speak in front of large crowds and terrifying to think about. I thought those days were over.

That first year after 9/11 when I spoke, I was a different person. It wasn't even me who was speaking; it was the Holy

Spirit speaking through me. But now I was just Shelly, and I knew I wasn't capable. I didn't want to go back to that painful place again, or allow myself to be so vulnerable. Besides that, there was no way I could speak at Cottonwood on 9/11 because Jacqueline and I were going to New York for the tenth anniversary.

I quickly declined that invitation from Jeana, though I also told her I would pray about it and maybe God would change my mind. Honestly, however, I had no desire to even pray about it because my mind was already made up, and I was secretly afraid that God was going to tell me something different from what I wanted to hear. Reluctantly I started praying about it, asking God to show me where I was supposed to be on 9/11.

Immediately God started working on my heart, and I knew exactly where I was supposed to be. I knew it was God's will for me to be at Cottonwood Creek on 9/11, but I had no idea what I was supposed to talk about. What did they want me to say? It had been ten years, and that part of my life was over. I couldn't talk about the beautiful love story between Steve and I, since I was happily married to another wonderful man. I was so confused. Why was God bringing me back to this place again?

I started looking for answers in the only place I knew to look: God's Word. I was looking for some sort of wisdom, asking God to show me what He wanted me to share. God's words jumped off the page and spoke to me as if He were standing in the same room speaking aloud:

> I pray that your hearts will be flooded with light so that you can see something of the future he has called you to share. . . . I pray that you will begin to understand how incredibly great his power is to help those who believe him. *(Ephesians 1:18–19 TLB)*

That was it! It was so simple. He just wanted me to tell my story, the story of how great His power had been in my life—how I'd relied on His promises, and how He'd carried me through the darkest days of my life and given me a hope and a future.

At the service at Cottonwood Creek on September 11, 2011, God once again was glorified through Steve's testimony and his short life here on earth. On this day, God planted a seed in my heart to tell my story, a seed that would grow and eventually become this book.

It has now been almost eighteen years since 9/11, and I'm not the same person I once was. It was in the midst of my darkest storm that I found out who I was and what I really believed in. My faith became so real.

In this world, we will have troubles. Being a Christian doesn't mean we're exempt from pain and suffering. It simply means we will not have to face our trials on our own. Through my own personal tragedy, I've felt a closeness to God that I believe I would never have known without going through such intense heartbreak. In my lowest of lows, I've felt God's presence, His peace, and His perfect love. Day after day, He used the pain in my heart to draw me closer to Him.

I'm in awe of the God I serve—the one who reshaped my destiny after my life was shattered into pieces and who put all those pieces back together and made me whole.

There are so many broken people in this fallen world we live in—all in need of hope. I know that kind of brokenness. I've been there! And I know without a shadow of a doubt that our only hope is found in Jesus Christ:

There is salvation in no one else! God has given no
other name under heaven by which we must be saved.
(Act 4:12 NLT)

My prayer for you is that you may know Him and the power
of His resurrection!

ACKNOWLEDGMENTS

Writing this book has been a long journey, and I am so thankful for all my friends and family who encouraged me along the way. Thank you for letting me pour out my heart to you as you listened to me read, helped me edit, learn new computer programs, and tried to make complete sentences. But most of all, thank you for praying for me and for this book. Anyone who knows me well knows this book is truly a miracle and God completely has His hand on it. I have learned that God does not ask if we are capable, He asks if we are willing.

A heartfelt thank you goes out to my husband, Heath, as well as to Honey, Papa, Big Mama, Karen, Robin, Niki, and my Bible study. His blessings have been made new to me each day by the precious people He has placed in my life. I am beyond blessed for your love and your prayers!

Shelly

52267664R00098

Made in the USA
Lexington, KY
10 September 2019